To Alison from R.D. Kernohan
with

Joh.

THE
PROTESTANT
FUTURE

THE
PROTESTANT
FUTURE

A Personal View
by
R.D.Kernohan

Christian Focus Publications

© 1991 R.D.Kernohan
ISBN 1 871 676 54 1

Cover design by Seoris N. McGillivray.

Published by
Christian Focus Publications Ltd,
Geanies House, Fearn IV20 1TW
Ross-shire, Scotland, UK

Printed in Great Britain by
Billing & Sons Ltd, Worcester

CONTENTS

OTHER BOOKS BY R.D.KERNOHAN
(Editor, Life and Work 1972–90).
Scotland's Life and Work (Saint Andrew Press 1979).
William Barclay, The Plain Uncommon Man (edited,
Hodder and Stoughton 1980).
Our Church: A Guide to the Kirk of Scotland (Saint
Andrew Press 1985).
Thoughts through the Year (Pentland Press 1985).

VOTES OF THANKS

It will be self-evident that this is a very personal book. Although many people are mentioned and a number quoted, the use made of their ideas and the context in which their words are set is very definitely my responsibility and not theirs.

I am especially grateful to those who responded to questions and inquiries from me, despite the warning that they might be quoted. I think the warning was clear enough, for one very senior politician took sufficient account of it to write me a very kind and fulsome letter of good wishes explaining that he was too busy to answer even two brief queries about the future of Protestantism. Those who did respond greatly helped and stimulated me. But the argument of the book, the conclusions, and the interpretation put on quoted material are mine alone.

I owe a special debt to the publishers for encouragement, guidance, and practical help, as well as for allowing me to set out this personal view. Some of what I say they would doubtless say differently and some of it they might not say at all! But I am grateful for their Christian understanding of the liberal conservative standpoint from which I write about the future of Protestantism. To many theological conservatives it will seem dangerously or naively liberal, though I trust that to radicals and the present liberal establishment it may seem not merely conservative but reactionary. There is a time to react against foolish leadership and bad advice.

To the Kirk of Scotland I owe most of my knowledge of the means of grace and hope of glory, as well as of the ways of God's Church. It will be clear that some of its leaders have influenced me through their teaching and good example, and others because I have reacted strongly against them. Indeed I reacted so strongly to their leadership of the Kirk into by-ways and blind alleys that I decided it was best for the Kirk that I should leave its professional service, after a happy and extended term as editor of *Life and Work*, a little earlier than I might have done. But that concentrated my mind wonderfully and directed my thoughts to this book, which is hardly at all about the political matters I have aired elsewhere. I remain grateful to my friends on both sides of the Kirk's various great divides.

My emphasis that the conclusions drawn from information and assistance received are entirely my own applies with special force to those in other Churches who have helped me. I am very grateful, for example, to the Rev. Tom Connelly, director of the Catholic Press and Media Office in Scotland, who helped me on some points connected with Roman Catholic law and practice on inter-communion.

I hope the book itself makes clear my view that even very profound disagreements can be faced and expressed in a Christian spirit and even with what the great Calvinist confession in English calls (in the section on communion of the saints) 'communion in each other's gifts and graces'.

R.D. KERNOHAN
Edinburgh, February 1991

1

WHAT FUTURE?

I have taken a risk with the title 'The Protestant Future'. It contains a deliberate ambiguity but it also invites a sceptical retort: 'What future?'

Many years ago I found myself debating in the Oxford Union against a singularly eloquent Jesuit. I was proposing a motion none too complimentary to the Roman Church and he was one of the two distinguished guest speakers, the other being Dr. Marie Stopes, the family planning pioneer. He was also, as it happened, a Scot, proving that the lad o' pairts can get ahead in any company; but he was far from being either a canny Scot or a taciturn one. The eloquence gushed out, not so much as from a tap as from some uncontrollable natural geyser, culminating in a prophecy that Protestantism would be extinct in England by the end of the century. He had at least the grace to say England, not Britain.

I dare say my compatriot never expected the heretic opposite to remember the prophecy the morning after the debate, never mind nearly forty years later. But it has worried me ever since, not only in relation to England, Anglicanism, and the diminished influence of 'Nonconformity' but to almost all the countries of what was once the Protestant part of Christendom, Scotland included. Almost everywhere the mainstream Protestant Churches appear to be shrinking in numbers or self-confidence or both: in Western Europe, the United States, even in Scotland where year by year the rolls of the Kirk fall steadily, with no statistical recovery in sight or even in middle-distance prospect.

It is no consolation that Father Joseph Christie's take-over train is running a bit behind his rhetorical schedule, or that some other trends have not quite travelled on the lines he expected. The only time his eloquence was even partially staunched that night was when he made the mistake of accusing Dr. Stopes of engaging in 'an infamous traffic' and was pulled up by the chair, whose tenant that term was Jeremy Isaacs, later of Channel Four and Covent Garden. Since the 1950's many things have gone Dr. Stopes' way rather than Father Christie's. Even the laity of the Roman Church seems to have been largely converted to her views. But it could still be argued, in a way that might carry conviction with the indifferent and the sceptical, that in so far as organised Christianity has any future at all it must rest with the apparently more determined and coherent big battalions of the Roman Catholic Church, well commanded by Popes John XXIII and John Paul II and not yet seriously undermined by the scattered mutinies of feminist nuns, Latin-American Marxists, and freethinking academic theologians.

Moreover in parts of the world where Christianity has spectacularly and successfully outlasted the Marxist-Leninist system which persecuted it and sought to extinguish it, the Roman Church can reasonably claim some of the credit, for courage, endurance, and the organisation of survival in a way that allowed it to take the opportunity for revival. It was Poland which first successfully defied Communism and then overthrew it in a peaceful revolution, and Roman Catholicism can claim to have avoided the mistakes by which most Orthodox and some Protestant leaders had sometimes compromised themselves with Communist régimes. Even in China it looks as if in the long run the persecuted Romanists will prevail over the 'patriotic Catholics' sponsored by the régime and apparently separated from the Vatican.

Such a view seems to have an appeal to the media, even in countries where the dominant cultural tradition is a Protestant one. Very often the Roman Catholic Church is meant when the phrase 'the Church' is used. Increasingly even agnostic journalists refer to the Pope and the papacy not only with a respect rarely allowed to secular leaders and institutions but in terms which implicitly (if sometimes unwittingly) accept Roman definitions on matters of Christian dispute: expressions like the Supreme Pontiff, the Holy Father, and the seven sacraments pass unrebuked by editors, while the Christian doctrine of the Virgin Birth of Jesus becomes hopelessly entangled with the Roman one of the Immaculate Conception of his mother.

At the same time there are powerful forces and significant trends within the Protestant Churches which also seem to raise questions not just about the nature of Protestantism's future but whether it has a future at all. It is comparatively rare to see the Anglican Church explicitly referred to as a Protestant Church. Those of its senior leaders who are themselves unimpeachably Protestant tend to emphasise their Anglicanism in the interests of the unity of their own communion. Dr. Robert Runcie never to my knowledge referred to himself as a Protestant Archbishop of Canterbury. Dr. George Carey, his successor there, seems to me a good Protestant as well as an Anglican but like many Continental Protestants is happier with the description 'evangelical'. Meanwhile ecumenical bodies, including councils of Churches whose roots and styles are unmistakably Protestant, refer to themselves — the World Council of Churches for example — as including Protestant, Anglican, and Orthodox Churches. It is not only Roman Catholics, unaware of the offence their terminology can cause, who refer to 'Non-Catholics' when they mainly mean Protestants.

At one time the ecumenical movement seemed to offer hope of a reconciliation and union of many Protestant groups before they faced together the far more difficult task of a dialogue on equal terms with Rome, but such a hope seems no longer tenable.

Internal Anglican debates, for example over the ordination of women, are conducted with many speakers looking over their shoulders to Rome and others making clear their preference for hypothetical unity with Rome to the long-established reality of co-operation with other Protestant Churches. At least lip-service to the possible 'primacy' of the Bishop of Rome comes from leaders who consider themselves middle-of-the-road Anglicans, even if the primacy they offer to accept remains very different from the authority the papacy demands. An Archbishop of Canterbury can speak of this primacy as if it raised no fundamental principle. When the Pope visited England Dr. Runcie was happy to concentrate the ceremonial of reconciliation around the memory of one martyred but turbulent archbishop, Thomas Becket. He did not risk the more awkward questions raised (despite the more profound reconciliation which might have been achieved) by an encounter in Oxford where Thomas Cranmer recanted his recantation and went to his martydom affirming a Protestant view of the Lord's Supper.

The Anglicans' flirtation with papal primacy and their reluctance even to think of themselves as Protestants at all is the most serious threat to Protestantism's future, if we think in terms of statistics and traditional spheres of influence. But even in other Protestant Churches curious speculations have been known about the 'Petrine ministry', a euphemism which has no point unless it is assumed that Peter was the first bishop of Rome and that this has some special significance for the whole Church.

Within the ecumenical movement, whose tone and style are still largely set by liberal Protestantism and its Third World derivatives, there is an emphasis on seeking formulae which will narrow the gap between the Roman system and Protestant practice. Understandably, the emphasis on things which we hold in common − for example in the idea of an ordained ministry and in our understanding of Communion and baptism − subtly moves to an attempt to redefine Protestant doctrine and amend Protestant practice. This is especially marked in the *Baptism, Eucharist, and Ministry* report of the WCC and it is implicit in a string of failed attempts to create more 'organic unity' in the Church by inducing Churches which don't have bishops to 'take episcopacy into their system'. Even when it is argued that this should be done on purely pragmatic grounds − because the Anglicans can't join in without episcopacy − this draws the argument closer to Roman Catholic assumptions. If you accept bishops from motives of pragmatism and expediency you can expect soon to be under persuasion to do something similar in relation to the Pope. If the Romans won't give up the papacy, and organic unity is imperative, the pressure is on to accept the office in principle and seek a satisfactory measure of ambiguity about what that acceptance actually means. The attempt may fail but while it lasts it is debilitating and a diversion from positive preaching and evangelism. And almost all the ill-effects will be felt on the Protestant side.

It is therefore perfectly reasonable to ask whether Protestantism has a future. Even if the answer is 'yes', it is reasonable by virtually all human standards of judgment and assessment to suggest that it is a very uncertain and not very influential future. Moreover the Protestant future is also bound to be affected by the very obvious differences among Protestants, not only because historic denominations tend to be more tenacious than ecumenists want them to be, but because of the deeper differences that have emerged between liberals and theological conservatives, often running to radical abandonment of the historic faith on one side and a narrow but fiercely assertive fundamentalism on the other. The Protestant future might seem not only uncertain but unpromising.

But it is God's promises that count. This survey seeks not only to assess the Protestant future, meaning the future of Protestant Christianity, but to suggest that what lies ahead for the worldwide Church is a Protestant future. That does not necessarily mean some dramatic statistical revival of the Protestant Churches in the West. It does mean that these Churches could move from survival to revival of various kinds; and it means that the worldwide Church will increasingly reflect some of the Protestant discoveries about the nature of the Church and, even more important, about the relation of God and humanity, to which the key is found in Jesus Christ, the only Head of the Church.

What Future?

I think of another Oxford prophecy, spoken in less congenial and more harrowing circumstances than those of the union debate I mentioned but just a couple of hundred yards away, at the corner of Broad Street outside Balliol College. Two bishops, Protestant colleagues of Cranmer, were being burned for their doctrinal errors in the eyes of Rome. I don't suspect the modern papacy of stockpiling faggots for use when the good times return; indeed I note that heretics with more radical views than Ridley or Latimer can only be sacked with great difficulty today from Roman Catholic institutions. As I write, I have the views on my desk of a lady described as Professor of Feminist Theology at a Dutch Catholic University. I am sure that even she is not for burning. But I want to set my argument in a broader context than that of a thrawn and stubborn Scots Presbyterianism, for Ridley and Latimer should be as dear to us as Patrick Hamilton and George Wishart; and I want to borrow one of the noblest and aptest metaphors in the English language.

This is how John Foxe, author of the great *Book of Martyrs*, rendered Hugh Latimer's words: 'Be of good comfort Master Ridley and play the man. We shall this day light such a candle by God's grace in England as I trust shall never be put out.'

The candle flickers, but by God's grace will not be put out: and not in England only. Wherever the Christian Faith has taken root men and women will ask the questions, and receive the answers from God, which led such Reformers in one age and culture to shape the tradition we call Protestant. I do not call it the Protestant Faith, for it is the Christian Faith, and only matters because it is Faith in Christ. In future times and other places those who encounter Grace in this way may not call themselves Protestant. Many of them will stay within Churches of other traditions. But the light will shine.

There is another fiery metaphor. It was much favoured as the Scots Reformed Kirk remembered in its prosperity the times when Presbyterianism was persecuted. But the Scots are said to have got it from the French Huguenots. In any event they both got it from the Old Testament and Moses' encounter with the bush that burned but was not consumed. Today, as the Scots Kirk encounters harder times in an unpropitious cultural climate, it may recover the full force of the metaphor. God will have surprises in store for the hedonistic and apathetic West, just as there were for the Eastern European countries in which atheism had been established as the State irreligion.

Today it may seem in much of the world, and especially the old Protestant heartland of the West, that the Churches of the Reformation inheritance are being shrivelled up. But they will no more be consumed than were the Churches under Communism. The truth they embody will not cease to be the truth. Some will guard it and many others will find and share it.

The Reformation inheritance will not be consumed. The candle will not be put out. And it ought, if we respond to a similar figure of speech used by Jesus in his teaching, to be put up where everyone can see it. There is a Protestant future as well as a Protestant inheritance. If we look to the Light of the World we shall see it shine through all the Protestant divisions, uncertainties, and dilemmas that are so apparent today.

2

CHRISTIAN, PROTESTANT, AND CATHOLIC

You cannot be a Protestant without first being a Christian. Neither the act nor the mood of protest has virtue in itself. Any virtue comes from the moral imperative to protest against something which is evil or, better and more positively, to proclaim the truth. That, for Protestants, is the Christian Faith, which asserts that Jesus Christ was not just a good man and important teacher but has a unique place in time and eternity which we describe by calling him the only Son of God. The Word, we say (quoting from the beginning of John's Gospel) became flesh and dwelt among us. And God so loved the world that he gave his only Son, so that everyone who believes in him should not perish but have everlasting life. These Christian beliefs are not exclusively Protestant but they are the heart of Protestant faith.

You can have Protestant attitudes, a Protestant background and inheritance, even proclaim Protestant slogans, certainly belong to a community so influenced by such background and attitudes that it might reasonably be called a 'Protestant community'. But without the Christian faith 'Protestant' is not only a word loose in meaning but emptied of its real meaning. Those who first were called by the name — followers of Martin Luther protesting against restrictions imposed by a German imperial diet in 1529 on reformed Christianity — wanted to preach the truths they thought they had discovered or recovered.

A few years before Luther had preceded the famous words attributed to him about refusing to budge ('Ich stehe hier, ich kann nicht anders') with a positive explanation of why he had to seem obstinate. 'My conscience,' he said, 'is captive to the Word of God.' His stand was not an act of self-will but of conscience, faith, and loyalty to a supreme standard. He had to become a protester because he was a Christian. And the Bible was the source-book and guide book for his Christianity.

Those who assert their Protestantism against what they see as errors in the Roman Catholic Church can only do so in the right mood and with the right objectives if they remember that you cannot be a Protestant without first being a Christian. There are times when we not only need to remind others of that: we also need to remind ourselves.

It should also be apparent in this century that the protest on behalf of Gospel truth and the Lordship of Christ, the one mediator between God and humanity, does not only require to be firmly and courteously sustained against some claims of the Roman Catholic Church. In face of Communism, with its Marxist and atheist ideology, consciences had to be captive to the Word of God. So too they must be in face of far gentler and more insidious challenges to Christianity, even of other religious faiths which often teach virtues and morality and testify to the human longing to discover the God whom Christians believe has revealed himself.

But there is another reminder needed. To Protestant

Christians it should be no more than a reminder. To other people it may come more as a surprise, and to many Roman Catholics and even Eastern Orthodox Christians it may sound somewhere between a surprise and a challenge, though there is no need for it to be a provocatively hostile one. You cannot generally be a Protestant without first being a catholic.

That is, you cannot be a Protestant without being a Christian; and you cannot readily lay claim to to the title of Christian without adhering to the universal or catholic Church and its doctrines, which means sharing its experience. Your faith is strenghthened by the example of others as well as shared with others. Protestants set the Word of God above human traditions, even those embodied in their Church. That does not mean they have no sense of tradition and no proper respect for the traditions of the Church. Far from it. Where these traditions (including those of the early Church and the Middle Ages) are an expression or distillation of Christian experience in response to God's Word they must not only be properly respected but profoundly cherished. That is a quite different matter from allowing an authoritarian Church to interpret its history and traditions, often the work of human ingenuity rather than divine inspiration, as if they were the expression of the Word. That respectful but critical view of tradition in the Church is the essence of Protestantism. It is positive and constructive, not negative and destructive, and it matters far more than any attitudes to styles, forms, and ceremonies in the Church or the arguments for and against particular forms of Church government.

Protestants are not inclined to set too much store by particular forms and ceremonies, and in a universal Church drawn from the entire human race and its many cultures these forms are bound to differ anyway. And to be honest, Protestants have in the past argued a lot among themselves about such things. They continue to differ about them, though most of the differences now can be seen as differences of custom, taste, tradition, and temperament rather than vital questions of faith and Christian obedience. But many Protestants affirm their faith during a service by saying together one of the creeds summarising the faith of Christians, usually the short one known as the Apostles' Creed which includes the phrase: 'I believe in the holy catholic Church'.

But Protestants believe in the holy catholic Church whether they choose to include such a formula in their services or not; and they belong to that Church. They believe that this Church is best ordered (though still very fallible) where it has been shaped by the ideas and insights which the Reformers recovered and applied — mainly but not only the great Reformers of the sixteenth century and those who have followed their traditions. The Church has always to be open to reformation. There were great reformers in the Church before the Reformation — some of them, like the Waldensians of the Alps and the followers of Jan Hus in Bohemia, really precursors of the Reformation and subsequently merging its traditions with those of Luther and Calvin.

This holy catholic Church, however, is more than an organisation. In some vital ways it is not an organisation at all, for it is possible to speak of both a visible Church — organised, though not necessarily united, far less regimented — and an invisible Church. That 'invisible Church' consists of all Christians and its only head is Jesus. It is best seen not just as only those Christians (regardless of denomination) alive in the world at any one time but as a wider union under Christ including those who went before us in the faith and those who will follow after us.

There is also a visible Church. It is visible as an institution and we also use the same word (perhaps without the capital letter to make a distinction) for the building which is both the sign and the home of a local part of the Church. It is visible too in the organisation of national and denominational Churches, large and small, and in the complex network of Christian communities which cover the world and cross all barriers of race, language, social structure, and educational background.

You cannot readily be a Protestant without seeking to be part of this catholic or universal Church, visible and invisible. The great English-speaking summary of Reformed belief, the Westminster Confession (so called because drawn up there in the seventeenth century) says that outside the visible Church 'there is no ordinary possibility of salvation', a sweeping statement which is perhaps helped by that happy note of reservation, which recognises that God is infinitely wiser than those who claim to be his vicars on earth. But in many of its other definitions of the role and nature of the Church the Westminster Confession of Faith (accompanied by useful but now rather neglected Larger and Shorter Catechisms) is both a profound and a profoundly realistic document and far more suited to modern needs than most of its critics allow. Too many people dwell too much on the one section of the Confession which adds a highly debatable (and in my view untenable) deduction from Scripture to a necessary denial of the claim that the Pope of Rome can be 'in any sense' head of the Church. It does not follow, in rejecting that claim, that we need to identify the office, never mind the man or (some day perhaps) woman who holds it, as

19

antichrist, man or woman of sin, and son or daughter of perdition. It is enough to affirm that Christ is sole Head of the Church and that any system which obscures that truth or contrives some auxiliary system of mediation falls short and opens the way for human error to become confused with divine purpose.

But the Reformed or Calvinist assessment of what the catholic Church is comes across essentially as a positive one, and in the true sense as an ecumenical one. The purest Churches under heaven 'are subject both to mixture and error', it says. It is hard for any Christian with a sense of history or realism to come to any other conclusion. We have only to look at the history of our own denomination, whatever it may be.

The catholic Church, meaning the institutions which compose it, 'has been sometimes more, sometimes less visible.' It is hard to look at the history of Christendom and not be struck by the different moods in different centuries and places (much more striking in some ways than mere denominational differences) as the Church tries to show the face and the faith of Christ. It sometimes succeeds. It often fails. And it has only too often distorted it.

Because the Protestant Reformation sought mainly to reform the Church within the boundaries of each State it automatically found itself recognising that the universal or catholic nature of the Church went with much diversity in practice, starting with the obvious and necessary diversity when services, including preaching, prayers, and the two sacraments of baptism and the Lord's Supper, were in the language of the people. There were others kinds of diversity, in Church government and in doctrine, which even Protestants took rather longer to accept in theory though they learned quite early to live with them in practice. Even now much ecumenical effort and energy are hopelessly diverted into efforts to create a common structure or 'order' for the Church.

But for all its own 'mixture and error' Protestantism never lost its sense of a universal Church. Nor did it necessarily exclude those who were not Protestants by happy accident of birth or geography. Even when the Westminster Confession speaks of 'synagogues of Satan' — a fine bit of alliterative rhetoric — it is because Churches have 'degenerated'. The claim about degeneration does not exclude the hope and possibility of regeneration. Indeed the Roman Church admitted a good deal of degeneration when it tried to put its house in order at the Council of Trent, though unhappily it ordered it in a way which widened the gap which opened up when the Reformation was checked in much of Europe. There has never been a time when Protestants in general failed to recognise that in the Providence of God much Christian virtue, piety, and scholarship flourished in the Roman Church and the Orthodox Churches.

The visible Church, as Protestants and other Christians believe, seeks to be the house and family of God on earth. It must therefore try to live as befits that house and family. It gathers together those throughout the world who 'profess the true religion' — in the Westminster Confession's phrase — and it therefore has to attempt some definition of what that essence of Christianity is. The creeds are no more than brief summaries and themselves are derived from interpretation of the Bible, which Protestants have always placed above tradition, for some traditions could be no more than constant repetitions of errors or misunderstandings. This visible Church also organises a ministry (which means a service to meet the needs of God's people), provides education in the Christian life, and offers what the modern world would call social services.

The 'catholic Church' is the whole body of Christians who seek these aims and embody them in communities and forms of worship. 'Catholic' means general, as distinct from local, so it refers to the universal Church as distinct from local congregations. Historically the word also has a doctrinal meaning, being applied to the body of the Church which defined and rejected various heresies and recognised a catholic faith. But this is the faith of the Bible and the creeds, not the organisation which came to be headed by the Bishop of Rome in the Western part of this universal Church. Eastern Christendom, though convinced it was truly catholic in doctrine, came to call itself Orthodox.

The Churches of the Reformation, commonly called Protestant, maintain they are both orthodox and catholic. They believe in a Trinity of Father, Son, and Holy Spirit, different persons of the One God. They believe Jesus is the 'only Son' of God, Son that is in a uniquely special sense; that he was crucified, died, and rose again. Along with Roman Catholics and the Orthodox they share the doctrines declared in the creeds, probably often listed there because some powerful heresy set out to deny them. But unlike many people in these other sections of the universal Church they affirm that tradition and even the creeds derive their authority and respect from the extent to which they reflect the Word of God as contained in the Bible.

Much of this study is about the difficulties which modern Protestant Church organisations encounter and even create in seeking to find, retain, and express this true catholicity. They can be too unsure what it means today to be orthodox and they are sometimes drawn in the wrong direction in trying to persuade others to accept them as catholic. But they have never been anything else.

Indeed it is only in the essentially Protestant belief in the right of private judgment, the priesthood of all believers, and the captivity of conscience to the Word of God that there is a proper bridge between the visible and invisible Church. It is wrong to distinguish between them too sharply. There is a danger (to which Protestants as well as Roman Catholics and Orthodox have yielded at times) to treat the visible Church as if it had a glory and authority that Christians must allow to God and Christ alone. But there is also a danger of retreating into the piety of small groups which see themselves as no more than tiny outposts of the invisible Church. The Protestant future needs have a sense of the Church catholic, past, present, and future, with a sense of achievement, mission, and trusteeship.

3

REFORMATION

There is reformation and there is the Reformation. Protestants should be concerned with both, respect both, understand both.

Christians are bound, by the changes in culture and society, to keep re-forming the Church. The effects of original sin on Christians themselves also demand a good deal of personal re-forming and recurring reformation if the Church is not to reflect the corruption and distortion which creep into individual Christian lives. Unfortunately the influences of culture, society, and the sum total of so many individual sins can produce not reformation but deformation. This has happened in many places and, to some degree, at all times in the history of the Christian Church. It is happening today, not only to one part of the Church or the disciples of one school of theology. It is bound to happen even when ingenious men, among them many pious Christians, construct a theology which tries to confer on the institutional Church the infallibility of the God who instituted it.

Such corruption happened very conspicuously in the Middle Ages, to the Church in general and to the papacy in particular. Although this is emphasised in traditional Protestant histories of the Reformation, for example when they deal with Martin Luther's righteous evangelical fury at the sale of pardons or 'indulgences', it is not the heart of the matter. Nor is an interpretation of what happened in the Middle Ages at the centre of the considerable differences that even today separate Rome from other Christians. The faith that was expressed by the builders of Salisbury Cathedral or Chartres or York Minster or Iona Abbey had at its heart something pure and noble that expressed the majesty of God, even if it was often sorely lacking in a sense of the uniqueness of Christ. The Church was re-formed, not rediscovered, in the sixteenth century and it inherited a legacy of piety and devotion more significant than the personal corruption of several Popes, the absurdities of relics (of which the bogus Turin Shroud still attracts the credulous even in our century), or the odd mixture of hypocrisy, lechery, and domesticity which existed along with the nominal celibacy of the clergy.

Protestants believe that the gulf between what the Church preached and what many of its leaders practised helped people to appreciate the rediscovery of essential truths about the Gospel and the Church itself. Roman Catholics do not dispute that there was much corruption and a need for reformation, though they maintain that Protestants went about it in the wrong way, broke the unity of the Western Church – the Eastern Church had long since separated in its organisation – and cut themselves off from the divinely instituted authority of the Church, of which they say the papacy is a vital part. Rome claims that it reformed and purified its part of the Church, and in some things and in its own ways it did.

At times Rome even seems to claim that Protestantism

was a punishment on the Church for the wickedness of Popes, worldliness among bishops, nuns who took their vows lightly, priests who bedded their housekeepers, and monks who feasted too well on Fridays. The process which involved the definition of Church doctrine and authority in ways unacceptable to Protestants (notably at the Council of Trent) also involved cleaning up the papacy and encouraging distinctively Roman styles of puritanism. The most spectacular, linking piety and militancy, was that of the Jesuits, inspired by Ignatius Loyola. He was a man with a personality as remarkable and intense as Luther's. The society which he founded may have been fanatical, ruthless, and at times devious but it was not hypocritical. Its members knew how to die well, whether as missionaries among the heathen or as political plotters against 'heretical' monarchs like Elizabeth of England and her successor James I (and VI of Scotland).

The sixteenth-century Reformation, and the Roman Counter-Reformation which reduced its territorial impact and at times threatened its survival, provided a stage on which powerful personalities could play dramatic roles. We are all also to some extent the inheritors of presentations of history which emphasised the role of personality. There is nothing wrong in that, even in understanding religious history. What a personality Paul must have had to win acceptance from a Christian community which was bound to suspect him! Theologians like Augustine and reformers like Benedict and Dominic had a remarkable impact not only on the Church but on the cultural history of Christendom. Teresa of Avila would have made a good Protestant and her practical brand of mysticism doesn't owe much to either good or bad Popes. Two centuries after the Reformation the same power of Christian personality in

John Wesley, thanks to the ill-judged response of his own Church of England, created a significant worldwide denomination and did much to shape the evolution of England.

It is not surprising that the traditional Protestant views of history emphasise the individual contributions of Martin Luther, John Calvin, John Knox, Ulrich Zwingli and others, as well as such precursors of the Reformation as the martyred Czech Jan Hus and the English 'morning star', John Wycliffe, saved from persecution by his powerful political connections. We need to guard against the uncritical hero-worship which accompanied much pre-twentieth century history and biography but when we do we shall still discover that the real spiritual stature of the great Reformers is undiminished.

This concept of heroic leadership has been most frequently associated with German Lutherans. In fact it is most emphatically and visibly demonstrated in the Reformation monument in Geneva, which conveys not only an impression of heroism but almost of hierarchy, as if all presbyters are equal but some (especially Calvin) rather more equal than others. Given the quality of Calvin's inspiration, that may not be the wrong impression to give.

This hero-worship was sometimes overdone in the past but the Protestant future necessarily involves understanding and appreciation of the past. This should neither be a blind and uncritical admiration nor a concentration on a few great names to the exclusion of far more numerous but humbler saints. It is a pity, for example, that the English-speaking peoples now so rarely read that classic *Book of Martyrs* by Foxe. Its virtues far outweigh any limitations, and it deserves to be ranked with *The Pilgrim's*

Progress after the Authorised Version of the Bible as a force for good in English history and a popular culture now all but lost in its own country. One of those virtues is its recognition that God speaks through and to simple people. The sixteenth century Reformation was not only shaped by men like Thomas Cranmer and William Tyndale, whose literary and spiritual greatness is still rather grudgingly acknowledged in a secular age, but by half-forgotten heroes like the Scots Lutheran Patrick Hamilton and by ordinary folk — weavers, or housewives, or shoemakers.

There is something especially grudging in the contemporary English and Scottish recognition of this Reformation inheritance, which is responsible not only for so much in our religious history but for our cultural and political evolution. Secular liberal, Roman Catholic, and Marxist historians have unwittingly forged an informal and unholy alliance to denigrate the Reformation, although careful reading of those who have real merits as historians often reveals unexpected affinity with traditional but now unfashionable Protestant views. I think for example of the Red Master of Balliol, Christopher Hill (a former tutor of my own) who even in his Communist days never quite escaped from the moral influence of one of his liberal Presbyterian predecessors, Sandy Lindsay. But agnostic historians have, not surprisingly, only a limited grasp of religious issues and cannot be expected to have the same spiritual priorities as evangelical Christians. Some very public reinterpretations of history have also owed something to political and diplomatic moods as well as ecumenical ones. Obvious examples are the way that the religious factor was deliberately played down in 1988 in the tercentenary celebrations of the Glorious Revolution and also in the 400th anniversary commemoration of the

Spanish Armada.

If something of the reputation of Cranmer and Tyndale has survived it is less because of their martyrdom or even of their spiritual achievement than because of their literary ones. Cranmer presided over the shaping of the English Book of Common Prayer and contributed much personally. Tyndale was not just a pioneer of biblical translation into English but the creator of much that helped shape the Authorised Version or King James Bible. But in Scotland John Knox has not had even this degree of justice done to him, because his literary achievement, *The History of the Reformation in Scotland,* (though it has some quite superb passages) has nothing like the same literary or cultural importance. Instead Knox has become the target for traditions of ill-informed criticism and a reaction which has been as much against Victorian Puritanism as the Reformation. Sometimes he gets credit which really belongs to others. Scots Presbyterianism as a system of church government probably owes more to the later reformer, Andrew Melville. Far more often Knox is blamed for every real or imagined fault of puritanism, mainly because of the way the romantic movement reacted to his quarrel with Mary, Queen of Scots. Schiller and a host of others got it all wrong.

Curiously, and more hopefully, Britain is probably the odd country out in Western Europe in this rather grudging attitude to its Reformation inheritance. If the Protestant future looks especially uncertain from a British viewpoint that is partly because we seem to have lost both our sense of history and our cultural bearings in the twentieth century, when we rapidly moved from being an overwhelmingly Protestant culture to becoming a largely secular and even agnostic one. A better understanding of the past helps to create a realistic appreciation of the future. Better examples abroad suggest that in time we may rediscover and cherish our history.

There are countries where the Reformation's victory was far less complete than it was in England or Scotland, or where the Counter-Reformation and political persecution put Protestantism's survival in danger, which seem to be more successful in doing justice to their heritage, and to their great reformers. They are not even all in Western Europe.

Czech Protestantism seemed to be wiped out in the seventeenth century. It survived underground and then revived along with the Czech sense of nationality, but never as more than a minority group. But even those Czechs who were Roman Catholic (or later Communist) cherished the memory of Jan Hus both as religious reformer and national hero. Now the Czechs have also rediscovered the role in their national life of another and far more modern national hero, their first President Thomas Masaryk, a man profoundly influenced by Protestantism as well as what is best in liberalism and nationalism.

In Hungary the Counter-Reformation reduced Protestants to a minority (today about 25 per cent, including many people with only a nominal adherence) but the history of Hungarian nationalism is very largely the history of Protestant leadership.

Switzerland has been fairly evenly divided in religion since the Reformation, though today there are more Roman Catholics than Protestants in the country as a whole. But each Protestant canton takes as much pride in its Reformation heritage as the Pope does in the turnout of his Swiss guards. There is a far better appreciation of such reformers as Farel and Zwingli than the average educated twentieth-century Scot has of Knox.

Despite its political predominance, Calvinism failed to convert large parts of the Netherlands. But even the secular and the large Roman Catholic section of Dutch society identifies with the great Protestant-led revolt against Spain and with the revolt's heroic leaders, especially William the Silent. Indeed Protestantism has so influenced the Dutch character that its modern Roman Catholics often seem to reflect the vices and uncertainties of liberal Protestantism (as well as some healthy scepticism about papal authority) rather than traditional Catholicism.

France has scarcely a million Protestants, and many of those belong to German-influenced traditions in Alsace. But the Huguenot tradition survived and no serious historian of French intellectual and religious history fails to recognise the stature of Calvin. Modern Roman Catholic scholarship takes him very earnestly and even in some things sympathetically.

If that is true of Calvin, who stands a bit apart from the dominant tradition in France, how much more true it is of Martin Luther in Germany. Long before its collapse the East German Communist régime had been forced to rehabilitate the most significant historical figure to belong to its territory. But Luther could not just be a local hero. He was the most significant figure not only in Reformation history but in centuries of German history. In translating the Bible he profoundly influenced the history of German as a language. For centuries the denunciation of him as a kind of antichrist went (at least in German Roman Catholicism) with a grudging recognition of his stature and perhaps a grudging admiration.

It is hard to find a parallel in the history of the English-speaking countries; and to convey something of the truth one has to go into flights of fancy. It is as if John Knox had the literary gifts and popular appeal of Robert Burns; or Shakespeare had taken time off from the Globe to give the King James Bible its literary style; or Cromwell had written Paradise Lost. Again the new atmosphere of intellectual freedom in Roman Catholic scholarship has attracted a lot of interest in a very Protestant hero. As with Calvin, the Roman Catholic historian or theologian may feel he has to take the line that it was a disaster (or a divine chastisement or whatever) that men with such insights and piety were separated from the Roman Church. That does not necess-arily stifle the admiration.

Luther will probably also gain a fresh importance in the German consciousness as the newly reunited Germany seeks symbols of unity. Like Goethe, he expressed some-thing of German nationality before that third and often less admirable hero, Bismarck, exploited nationalism to create a German State.

Is it unreasonable to hope that time and truth will ensure that England and Scotland will recover a stronger sense of the role in their history of such formidable and influential figures of such different Protestant styles and talents as Knox, Melville, Milton, Cromwell, and Bunyan?

4

CHRISTENDOM DIVIDED

It was not the Reformation but its partial failure which left the Western half of Christendom divided. The original universal or catholic Church had already for centuries been divided by schisms, mainly between East and West but also among some of the Eastern Churches too. Yet the sense of belonging to the universal Church was as strong in what, with benefit of hindsight, we call Protestantism as it was in the parts of the Church which remained Roman Catholic and were eventually regulated and in some things reformed by the Council of Trent which met between 1545 and 1563, more than a generation after Luther's great protest. In some ways that sense of universality was even stronger among the early Protestants. They hoped for a biblical re-formation of the Western Church and that the same light would spread eastwards and end the great schism between Latin and Greek forms of Christianity.

In Roman Catholic eyes that Council of Trent, which met on the great trade route over the Alps where Italian and German cultures touch, was the nineteenth general or ecumenical council of the universal Church. There was not to be another such gathering until 1869–70 when the first

Vatican Council added the infallibility of the Pope (within defined limits) to the other points on which Rome had rejected the Reformers' affirmation of the supremacy of Scripture. The view of grace, the sacraments, Church order, and ecclesiastical authority which the Reformers had derived from the Bible was rejected and it is only in the twentieth century that significant parts of the Roman Church have reopened their minds to at least some of these truths.

The sixteenth century Protestants had to argue, with some justice, that they wanted a general council — but not the kind offered at Trent. Luther in particular (who died the year after the council met) seems, to many modern scholars and admirers, not only one of the first great Protestants but the last of the great medievalists in his ways of thought and argument. Calvin, who died the year after the long council was completed, seems to belong not just to a different generation but to a different century.

In practice Luther, Calvin, their colleagues and successors, and Protestant leaders elsewhere had to adjust their plans and their thinking to circumstances. Luther was protected at crucial times not only by German public opinion but by political forces which were bound to shape the style of German Protestantism as well as the political future of what was then still called the Holy Roman Empire but is rather more comprehensible by the modern term of federal Germany. Elsewhere the most spectacular intrusion of political factors and ambitions into doctrinal arguments was the declaration of Church independence by King Henry VIII of England, a ruthless and dictatorial monarch who was hostile to the Lutheran influence but wanted to be his own Pope. He did not create the Church of England but did bring conditions in which it was separated from Rome and open to reform, especially under the influence of that scholar of questing mind and (until he was put to his last test) rather uncertain courage, Thomas Cranmer.

Human motives are always mixed and Christians are far from immune either to the simpler vices or the subtler ones. The vast material possessions of the medieval Church bred covetousness as its power began to crumble and human nature made it inevitable that Protestant doctrine often went with an eye to the main chance. In Scotland the first support for the doctrines of Luther and then Calvin among the upper classes was a matter of intellectual and spiritual conviction. The same could not be said of all those who joined the winning side.

Even where the Reformation went with a powerful current of practical idealism (as in Hugh Latimer's sermons or John Knox's plans for Scottish education) the pressures of the powerful either blocked or scaled down the plans of the Reformers. Luther himself discovered very quickly after his defiance of Rome and Emperor that an evangelical reformer could be out of his depth in politics, and forced towards a choice of evils in a time of civil conflict. It is even possible as early as the 1520's to see some of the later differences among Protestants between political conservatives and radicals, notably in the different lines taken by Luther and Thomas Münzer in face of the German peasants' revolt, when Münzer became a revolutionary and Luther (always with a weakness for the vigorously outspoken phrase) took the side of the existing social order.

Protestantism was inevitably a force for political and social change and sometimes a potential force for social revolution. But in these secular matters it became involved with tendencies which were already present. For example the cruel revolt and repression in Germany (where Luther was more compassionate than some of his words suggested) had been matched long before the Reformation in France and was to have its parallels in Russia long after it, and even in Spain, so little touched by the Reformation.

The intellectual ferment, release of energies, and perhaps redistribution of the assets vested in the medieval Church also stimulated economic change but it is best to be cautious about theories which link Protestantism with the rise of capitalism. Trends which might be called 'capitalist' were apparent in pre-Reformation Germany, Italy, and Flanders. We also ought to be cautious about the links, which do exist but can be complex and contradictory, between Protestantism and nationalism or the sense of nationality. Henry VIII played a nationalist card against Rome, and his daughter Elizabeth had to fight against Rome for her throne and even her life. Luther was (and remained) a German folk-hero. The Dutch fight for independence from the Spanish king's empire was eventually Protestant-led and came to be closely associated with the Calvinism which dominated the politics and religion of the northern provinces of the Netherlands.

But all these events tended to be interpreted by nineteenth-century historians in the light of their own times and ideas, many of which we have unconsciously inherited. If the Reformation came to be associated with the rise of nationality that was through circumstances rather than design. Luther's most determined critics were also Germans. A century after his time it took King Gustavus Adolphus of Sweden and a mercenary army (including many Scots) to check the German Catholic reaction. Calvin was a French intellectual whose example and influence came to be wielded through a city-state which became Swiss long after his time. But the Reformation was to divide the Swiss cantons themselves into Protestant and Catholic groupings. The coming of the Reformation to Bohemia cut across the old lines of national division there between Czechs and Germans. In the Netherlands Dutch Catholics tended to follow the Protestant lead of the House of Orange, but their Flemish cousins fairly soon settled quietly for Catholicism and foreign rule. In England Elizabeth had always to take account of a powerful Fifth Column among some (but not all) English Catholics. In Scotland John Knox and the Reformers deliberately chose the Auld Enemy instead of the Auld Alliance in order to safeguard the Reformation. As late as the early eighteenth century persecuted French Protestants were still in alliance with Britain against the French king. In the previous centuries they had vainly fought to gain control of the kingdom and then to remain as a kind of State within a State inside it.

In so far as it is possible to talk of 'wars of religion' following the Reformation they are very often civil wars within an ideological conflict. Indeed in the English, Scottish, and Irish civil wars mid-way through the seventeenth-century religious adherence and inclinations tended to be a determining factor. But there were many cross-currents, some changing of sides (as in the notable case of that National Covenanter, the Marquis of Montrose), and for a time dynamic new forces which emerged from within Protestantism were more important than the original religious divide left by the Reformation. Even in the sixteenth century Calvinism and the systematic 'Reformed' theology and order which it had created made Lutheranism seem fairly conservative in comparison.

Seventeenth-century England bred forms of Puritanism which left Calvinism in its traditional forms far behind. Cromwell emerged from 'independency' or Congregationalism to march towards an unplanned military dictatorship. John Milton, though suspected of taking liberties with doctrine, achieved the most astonishing literary synthesis of the biblical and the classical. And within the ranks of Cromwell's armies a variety of radical and utopian groups claimed an attention – at the time and from modern historians – out of proportion to their numbers. Meanwhile orthodox Calvinism had encountered and only temporarily subdued the challenge of a 'revisionism' named after Jacobus Arminius (alias Jakob Hermans in Dutch) which in some ways is the precursor of much modern Protestant evangelicalism, through its emphasis on free will and Christ's sacrifice of himself for all humanity.

The Reformers had set out to purify the one universal Church, which they recognised as a kind of loose confederation of Churches organised territorially in the realms of the various 'civil magistrates', as the Westminster Confessions calls kings. Like the great Protestant economist Adam Smith, they depended on the rationalising and reconciling power of an 'invisible hand'. In theory they waited for that general or ecumenical council of the Church which could not in practice meet, and in practice they used the astonishing network of contacts which scholars of the time maintained thanks to their command of Latin and despite the delays and unreliability of communications in the age of sail and saddle-bags. In time the Reformation created denominations – including the largest denomination, the papal one – but it also discovered Christian pluralism.

Arguably the Reformers also opened the way for a much wider pluralism in which the toleration which Christians found themselves extending to each other – often rather grudgingly – could not indefinitely be denied to others.

Protestantism did not so much preach tolerance as discover it through circumstances and even necessity, proceeding unevenly and by fits and starts. Some Protestants (like Catholics) were still frantically harrying witches while other Protestants were consciously breaking with medievalism in their toleration of Jewish communities. The greatest of Protestant painters, Rembrandt, drew some of his greatest inspiration from Jewish subjects and Cromwell formally revoked the exclusion of the Jews from England. Earlier Shakespeare had set out to write a very anti-Semitic comedy and found himself, in the humanism of Elizabethan England, dangerously close to sympathy with his Shylock — just as Milton at times seemed to be with his fallen archangel in 'Paradise Lost'.

These examples hint at some of the cultural and intellectual vigour which followed the Reformation. They are worth at least a passing mention if only to reject the contrast between a dark iconoclastic Protestantism and a colourful, vibrant Catholicism mingling ethereal Spanish visions of the Virgin with naked fat ladies from Rubens. In English, for example, the Reformation both reshaped and stimulated the literary language, with an astonishing range (to mention only very committed Christian writers) from Spenser and Milton to John Donne, the Protestant convert who produced what reads like twentieth-century verse from a seventeenth century deanery, and John Bunyan, who mapped out the ways of eternity among the sloughs and fairs and castles of the English landscape. English-speaking Protestantism never produced a musical tradition like the one in which Johann Sebastian Bach flourished (though it borrowed and encouraged Handel) but it did well in print.

But of course the achievement of the Authorised Version

of the Bible dwarfs everything else, setting the imagery of Scripture into the language of the people, putting the Gospels into a timeless narrative English, and letting the words of Christ and the letters of Paul speak with all the original freshness which made the early Christians ensure they were set down and passed on. But in every country touched by the Reformation the Bible became part of the culture of the people. The good ground was prepared for the seed. Much of it is still to be sown in the Protestant future.

5

REASON, REVOLUTION AND RECOVERY

It is always dangerous and misleading to divide history into neat segments, and especially the history of beliefs and ideas. The divisions have a certain validity when we arrange them around the comparatively few historical events about which we can honestly say that 'things could never be the same again'. There aren't many of them. The European discovery of America was one. The atom bomb on Hiroshima was another.

Even those few are sometimes recognisable only after a little time has passed. If the troops really had been home by Christmas we would certainly not reckon August 1914 in this way. Earlier in the year the murder of the Austrian Archduke Franz Ferdinand in Sarajevo hardly seemed likely to mark the end of an era. Luther's Ninety-five Theses nailed to the Wittenberg church door were recognisable as a turning-point in history only after events had moved dramatically on and the Saxon monk survived where Hus had perished. The Glorious Revolution of 1688 in Britain (subsequently seen as the security for civil and religious liberty and a decisive moment in constitutional history) was at risk for a few years afterwards in face of an inglorious reaction. And in 1789 (whatever Wordsworth may have said later) bliss was not instantly apparent, far less very heaven, just because a mob had stormed the Paris prison of the Bastille that was almost empty and in need of demolition. The wisest and profoundest of all reflections on the French Revolution, those of the Anglo-Irish Protestant Edmund Burke, seemed at the time to many people in Britain an extreme and far-fetched reaction to some sensible and hopeful developments in France, a nation of which not too much was to be expected anyway.

That warning is necessary when thinking and writing of the age of reason, or the 'Enlightenment', or even the American and French revolutions. It applies in the previous century when one writes of the 'end of wars of religion' or satisfies examiners by arguing that, somewhere during the Thirty Years War of 1618–48, what had begun as a conflict of Protestant and Catholic became a power-struggle in which a French Cardinal paid Lutheran Swedes to hire Scots mercenaries to fight in Germany. Most human motives are mixed and anyone allowed the Psalmist's span of seventy years lives through ages which history presents as contrasts but which overlap and interact.

But there are discernible and important trends in the eighteenth century which remain very relevant to the later history, present state, and uncertain future of some religious ideas and institutions. History does not repeat itself but it can produce some odd echoes from times past.

First, the Protestant and Roman Catholic divisions of Europe reached a way of living together in practice, even though set in their different ways. The second half of the twentieth century learned to call a slightly similar situation 'peaceful coexistence'.

Secondly, the different strands in Protestantism became

less alienated from each other, though the timidity and torpor of the Church of England led to the creation of a new offshoot of Anglicanism which had wider evangelical affinities and an Arminian theology: Methodism.

Thirdly, there emerged in different ways as well as different countries a concept of toleration which implicitly accepted the concept of religious pluralism. In France the fashionable writer, Voltaire, emerged as advocate for the persecuted remnant of the Huguenots, the proscribed French Protestants. In Austria the Emperor Joseph II tried to reshape his empire with explicit tolerance not only of Protestants but of other religious minorities, including Jews. In Britain (and even under harsher political and economic pressures in Ireland) Roman Catholics suffered civic disabilities rather than persecution. And across the Atlantic religious toleration and pluralism, already apparent in the foundation and development of different colonies, were written into the constitution of the United States formed from the thirteen colonies which declared and defended their independence.

But fourthly, some part of the tolerance seemed a reflection of relative indifference and laxity. The tone of the times — the equivalent of the ideas which dominate the media today — was often sceptical, though there was no clear dividing line between between belief and unbelief.

Take Voltaire, the sceptical French Catholic — Catholic that is in form, for the substance of his faith is closer to Deism than Christianity. But he is justly celebrated for one of his better deeds, his attack on the intolerance which in the Calas case had a Protestant father executed on the trumped-up charge of murdering his son to prevent him becoming a Roman Catholic. Voltaire vindicated Calas with great power. He was a major force in the gradual retreat by the reign of Louis XVI from the infamous persecution of Protestants associated forever with the name of Louis XIV and his revocation of the Edict of Nantes which had guaranteed their liberties when their political leader, Henry of Navarre, became King of France by conforming to Roman Catholicism. This was on the famous grounds that 'Paris is worth a Mass'. A curious by-product of this situation is that French historical research, when celebrating the bicentenary of the revolution of 1789, found a surprising amount of moderate royalism among the French Protestants of the time. More of them mourned Louis XVI when he went to the guillotine, it appears, than joined in the excesses of the revolution. Voltaire will also be found advocating tolerance on the dubious ground that in Alsace (where the persecution did not apply) other pressures to conform to the State religion of the French Crown were equally successful in converting the laxer and more worldly of the Protestants.

The eighteenth century's Deism cut across all the denominational lines established by the Reformation and its aftermath. There is little Christian in the Gospel sense about Voltaire and even less about Talleyrand, the bishop of the ancien régime who turned diplomat to serve the revolutionaries, Napoleon, and the restored Bourbons. But it is not easy to fit a literary genius like Goethe into the tradition of Martin Luther or (moving to Scotland) to put David Hume, the sceptical philosopher, into the intellectual lineage of John Knox and Andrew Melville.

In parts of Reformed Protestantism there was a slackening of doctrinal certainty and evangelical enthusiasm which came very close to presenting the Christian Faith as no more than the inheritance of a great teacher who expressed the will of a very abstract Supreme Being. Indeed in some parts of the Protestant world the Calvinists seemed especially susceptible to a drift which would have made Socinians or Unitarians of them. This was evident in such distinctively and at times assertively Protestant traditions as that of New England Congregationalism and Irish Presbyterianism. Survivals of this dilution of evangelical Protestantism can be found today in the traditions of Unitarianism on both sides of the Atlantic.

Similar moods can be found in Anglicanism, though there the torpor of establishment is more evident than a ferment of doctrinal reappraisal. Some of the piety of Anglicanism was diverted into the backwater of political 'non-juring', though at its best this tradition found a place in Christian history that was literary rather than political, for example in the hymns of Bishop Ken and later the *Serious Call to a Devout and Holy Life* by William Law. For the most part eighteenth-century Anglicanism – it is hard not to add, like some twentieth-century Anglicanism – seemed rather worldly and too ready to conform to political fashions of the day. It had its individualists like Laurence Sterne, author of *Tristram Shandy* and *A Sentimental Journey* and it gave a cool response to the most significant Church of England evangelical of the century, John Wesley, who no more wanted to set up a new denomination than Martin Luther wanted to create a new Church. Wesley was the Billy Graham of his day, for he spoke to people about sin and salvation, often reaching those who were unmoved by the regular ministrations of the Church. Had the Church of England been more innovative and flexible the Methodists might never have left it.

This is not the place to examine the complexities of eighteenth century religion in detail, and professional historians and specialists among them might object to the simplifications of the last few paragraphs. In Scotland, for example, the 'Enlightenment' produced a moderate party in the Kirk which made a notable contribution to Scottish intellectual history and which, among its virtues, was often responsive to new ideas and enthusiasms like those of Wesley. See for example the welcome and assistance which Wesley's diaries of his Scottish visits often record from ministers of the Kirk. Or study the background to the curious mixture of tradition, piety, rebellion, and satire which are found in the poems of the most remarkable Scots Presbyterian of the 'Enlightenment', Robert Burns.

But amid the complexities there is one tremendous and often neglected simplicity. In the eighteenth century there was much doubt, unbelief, scepticism and laxity. Religion sat lightly on many people who professed it and was sneered at by others. A sceptic of genius, Edward Gibbon — influenced, even perhaps soured, by his brief experience as a Roman Catholic convert — gave English literature its finest ironies at the expense of the Church.

Yet all of this antedated Darwinism and Thomas Huxley by a century. It emerged in a century whose ships were far closer to those of Drake and the Spanish Armada than to the age of steam. Its roads remained far worse than they had been in Roman times. Its battles were fought with cavalry, infantry, and ponderous artillery not vastly different in style from those of the seventeenth century.

Its industrial, medical, and agricultural revolutions lagged far behind the intellectual one which devalued religion. Its literature in England lacked the genius of Shakespeare — whom Voltaire appreciated so little — or the wonderful synthesis of the Puritanical and the classical in Milton. In France it lacked the sparkle of Molire or the sonorous elegance of Racine and Corneille. In architecture it had some achievements, but nothing to match the cathedrals of the Middle Ages or the Protestant serenity of Wren as seen in St Paul's Cathedral and the London City churches. Its art reached its highest quality in the portraiture of rather self-confident and even self-satisfied people who could afford the best artists. It saw itself as an age of order, improvement, harmony, and restraint; and it distrusted 'enthusiasm', not least religious enthusiasm.

Then it produced the tragic irreligious enthusiasm of the French Revolution, with all its aftermath for Europe of disorder, conflict, and destruction. Not for the first time – so those who remembered the biblical accounts of the Tower of Babel and the Flood might reflect – humanity had over-reached itself. It had been deluded by its own progress. In so far as the age was Deist and not merely sceptical it created a Supreme Being with a suspicious resemblance to its own philosophers. Humanity had been down that road before and was to take it again.

Such denunciations have, of course, to be qualified. Firstly, by that warning against neatly creating and chop-ping up ages of this and that – reason, revolution, reaction or whatever – for purposes of historical narrative and argument. Secondly, by appreciation that even in a cold spiritual climate there are always some hearts aflame with God's love or scorched by a sense of sin. There are always those, individuals or groups, quietly or turbulently going against the prevailing trend and temper and often coming into their own as events unfold and ideas or tastes change. A history of eighteenth-century piety would be neither simple nor brief. Nor was revival confined to the Wesleyan Methodist movement.

In England, for example, there was not only Wesley but the more Calvinist strain of George Whitefield. He too influenced Scotland. And in Scotland also Presbyterianism was either disturbed or enriched (according to one's point of view) by a series of secessions by those unhappy with the Kirk's handling of doctrinal matters or its relations with the State, or both. The most distinguished French Roman Catholic counter-attack on French philosophies of reason and scepticism, that of Chateaubriand, came from a man who was past thirty when the revolution came. He was only a few years younger than Robespierre and Danton, older than Napoleon Bonaparte, whose destructive ambitions wrought the bloody havoc our century associates with Hitler's.

Indeed the eighteenth-century age of alleged enlightenment has some resemblances to our own, not least in its pluralism. The most radical and the most traditional views of life, the most spiritual and the most secular, co-existed in the same countries and were part of the same civilisation: one that could plausibly be called neo-Christian.

The parallel should not be drawn too far. It does not follow from the similarities, for example, that each age of doubt, indifference, and revolutionary conflict will necessarily be followed by the same kind of evangelical revival. But there is guidance from the greatest single difference between that sceptical age and ours. The objections to God which one encounters today, the elevation of human wisdom, the concentration on hedonism and very worldly pleasures, and the rejection of any sense of sin: all these were to found in a civilisation whose most dramatic scientific and technological development still lay ahead. Our century has laboured with the notion that science has somehow 'disproved' religion, perhaps most crudely expressed when the Soviet professional atheists made much of Gagarin's assurance that he had not encountered God in the course of his space travels. The eighteenth-century sceptics were subtler and shrewder. They challenged God where he deserves to be most honoured, in the heart and mind of humanity. They appealed to human nature against divine revelation. It is an appeal that has always won a hearing.

Christians today differ on how God means us to read the account of the Creation, the Garden, and the Fall with which his Word begins. Let anyone who thinks that the account of the serpent, the Tree of Knowledge, and the temptation is no more than a fable reflect on its insights into human nature, and apply these insights to the arrogance, the temptation, and the misuse of the fruits of knowledge which marked the French Revolution in one century and the Russian one in ours. Man's first disobedience was not his only one.

But if Paradise was lost, and false paradises promised time and time again thereafter, it is also regained: not through human efforts but through God's grace, expressed and shown in Jesus. That grace does not mean that the Kingdom of Heaven will be established here as a temporal as well as a spiritual state, but it inspires and enables Christians to find and share the means of grace. It also encourages them to seek to maintain the piety, justice, and peace according to 'wholesome laws' whose maintenance the Westminster Confession lists among the duties of the civil magistrate. They remain our duties if we think in a more democratic age not merely of the individual monarch (which is what magistrate in the Confession means) but of the civil magistracy of constitutional government.

What stands out in the history of Western civilisation is the recovery of Christianity in the nineteenth century. It was a recovery which knew no denominational boundaries, and which crossed many geographical and cultural boundaries. The spiritual and social vigour of Christianity in Europe and North America went with its expansion in a missionary age: with great success in Africa and the Pacific; dramatic impact in India, China, and — in a late and hitherto neglected Victorian phase — in Korea; but chastening disappointments almost everywhere in the Islamic world.

In economic, technological, and social matters as well as spiritual ones it was a self-confident age but by no means the smug, complacent, or hypocritical one that it is sometimes represented to be. When we read Dickens we encounter not merely social criticism but the self-criticism of the age, among those who rushed to read him as well as in the author himself. It was an age not merely of emphasis on self-improvement but with a steadily growing passion for social improvement, both through 'wholesome laws' and personal or corporate philanthropy. Often this passion — as in Wilberforce's campaign against slavery or Shaftesbury's for social control of the new industrial forces — not only went with powerful Protestant Christian conviction but was inspired by it. This was especially the case of the foundation of youth movements such as the YMCA (and later YWCA) or the Boys' Brigade, the pattern for later uniformed organisations. And it was also the age which saw the Salvation Army as a spiritual and social response to the dark side of Victorian life.

The Victorian age achieved so much in so many ways that its main weakness was probably a belief in the inevitability of progress. It confused mere change with progress and wrongly assumed that moral improvements would come with technical ones or through the spread of popular education. The world was soon to know better.

6

THE LOST CENTURY

What went wrong in the twentieth century? It began aus-
piciously for Protestantism. Neither liberalism, Darwinism,
nor biblical criticism appeared to have shaken its ascend-
ancy in the modern world — for it seemed superficially to
have come to terms with all three — or its association with
forces which good Victorians would have called progress.
Phrases like 'social and Christian progress' shaped themselves in the mind as well as on the masthead of *The British
Weekly*, journal of the Nonconformist conscience in print.
There seemed to be a broad middle ground between the
extremes of reaction (exemplified in different ways by
Russian Tsarism and the papacy) and of Marxist Socialism.
The fashionable romanticism of the early and mid-
nineteenth century had encouraged a 'Catholic revival',
spectacularly associated with the defection of John Henry
Newman from the Anglican Church and also with the
influence of John Keble and Edward Pusey within it. Yet
long before the end of the century this drift towards Rome
seemed to be less important, taking Europe as a whole,
than a drift away from it. One could take a broader view
and find liberal Protestant values in the ascendant. Even

Socialists of the milder sort like the the Scots miners' leader James Keir Hardie seemed to find a place within that consensus. Had even he not had a poem published in the Scots Kirk's magazine: a bad poem, perhaps, but pious in its good intentions as well as its phraseology?

The Protestant ethic seemed, long after Wilberforce and Shaftesbury, still to inspire many of the more constructive and reasonable forces of change. A few years into the new century a very Presbyterian American college president (and son of the manse) called Woodrow Wilson was to exemplify them, first in New Jersey state politics, then in the White House, and then farther afield. But the Protestant ethic in a different variant seemed to harness and enlighten the most powerful forces of social conservatism and private wealth.

For the first time since the Reformation the Great Powers appeared to be more influenced by the Protestant view of the world than a Roman Catholic one. It also seemed possible, that as democratic forces became more influential, religious impulses might shape the forces of social and international change. Things were to turn out very differently but the Protestant optimism which now seems astonishingly naive (given the Christian view of humanity's fallen condition) appeared reasonably plausible in the first years of the twentieth century.

The three greatest Powers were predominantly Protestant countries: the German Empire or Reich, as reconstituted in 1871 by Bismarck and dominated by Prussia; the United States; and the British Empire. Each had a substantial Roman Catholic element but this was either eager to integrate with the dominant political culture (as in the United States); or largely associated with a minority ethnic tradition (as with the Irish of the British Empire); or (as in

Germany) still coming to terms with a comparatively recent realignment of power and influence. Moreover the self-confidence of German Catholicism had also been shaken by the enhancement of papal power and the declaration of infallibility at the Vatican Council, forced through in face of substantial German and Austrian opposition.

All three of these dominant powers, but especially the British and the Americans, were deeply involved in the world-wide export of European styles of Christianity. Christianity had just gone through a phase of expansion which appeared on the same scale as that of the earlier great missionary ages. The missionary successes and prospects of the late nineteenth century seemed to bear comparison with the early Church's spread across the Mediterranean, the conversion of Europe, and the Spanish and Portuguese achievements of the sixteenth century which created 'Latin America' and scraped a new Christian foothold in Asia.

Even those Great Powers most conspicuously outwith the Protestant tradition appeared to be making concessions to the temper of the times. France was dominated by secular Republicans with whom many Protestants found it easy to co-operate, while the Roman Church seemed often to be in a state of 'internal emigration'. Even in areas of French life where traditional Catholicism was strong, such as the army, there were grumbles that it was easier for Protestants and Freemasons to get promotion. Political Catholicism and its allies in the French army also suffered, often deservedly, from their involvement in the Dreyfus case, when a cruel mistake was turned into a conspiracy to pervert the course of justice.

In Austria the transition to 'Austria-Hungary' had weakened the Habsburg power so closely identified since the Reformation with Roman Catholicism, even when the

Emperor Franz-Josef got over his annoyance at the ultra-montane victory at the Vatican Council. The new set-up gave a disproportionate influence to the Magyars, many of whose nationalist leaders (the two Tiszas for example, as well as the exiled Kossuth) were Protestants. At the other end of the Habsburg Empire Protestant impulses could be found even in rival forces — for example in the emerging Czech movement whose most significant intellectual leader was Thomas Masaryk and in the pan-German nationalism which preferred the new Reich to the Habsburgs. Associated with that German mood was the 'Los von Rom' idea which, as the literal translation suggests, wanted to move away from the Vatican connection and clerical influence.

In Russia, which thought of Protestantism as a Western religion as well as a heresy, the old order was changing. Traditionally Germans and Balts had contributed much to the empire but had tended to be absorbed into the Ortho-dox Church (like German brides of the Tsars) when they approached positions of great power and influence. But Russia was stirring with new ideas, including freedom of conscience. Evangelicals in the West looked forward to a free Russia in which some old-established dissident tra-ditions might converge with Protestantism, as began to happen on a small scale with the Baptists.

Even in Italy, nominally admitted as a great European power, there were a few shoots of Protestant growth, while the political power of the papacy seemed to have been squandered in a futile quarrel with the lax or lapsed Catholics who set the liberal and anti-clerical tone of politics. The Pope was 'the prisoner of the Vatican', impotently protesting against Rome's absorption in the united Italy which the rest of the world concluded had come to stay.

Outside Europe (apart from the USA) there were few

signs of native power and influence. India looked a permanent part of the British Empire and its native élite seemed bound to be influenced by Christian missionary education. Japan baffled the late Victorians and Edwardians with its obvious ability to adapt to Western ideas and technology and its lack of interest in Christian missions, though those who wanted grounds for far-fetched hope were able to find them. In any event, Japan seemed far less significant in the long run culturally or economically than China. There at the turn of the century the Boxer Rebellion showed both the strength of hostility to Western influence – exemplified in Christian missions – and the existence of a small Chinese Church capable of surviving persecution and even facing martyrdom, along with missionaries who testified that they could die bravely as well as quarrel fiercely.

Meanwhile there was a 'scramble for Africa' among the Christian denominations and missionary societies as well as the colonial powers. It involved a vast amount of personal heroism and sacrifice, and often remarkable personal ministries, such as that of Mary Slessor in Nigeria. Even more significantly, Protestant missions took forms which promised to create relatively quickly an indigenous Christian leadership as well as a small educated class. This could not fail to have political influence, however circumscribed its prospects seemed to be in 1900, but it raised more immediate questions of African influence in the Church. There was a black bishop (Samuel Crowther) as early as 1864, though his career was accompanied by controversy. At about the same time the first black South African to become a Presbyterian minister (Tiyo Soga) was translating *The Pilgrim's Progress* into Xhosa. In the latter part of the nineteenth century there had been a more cautious approach — some modern critics call it a more racist one — but the foundations were laid for a policy of eventually self-supporting, self-governing, and self-propagating African Churches. The 'three-self' formula, later associated with post-revolutionary China and corrupted by political pressure, had its origin in the vision of Victorian missions. And it was in Africa that it appeared to bear most promise.

The new century promised to fulfil a much wider promise, but brought failures, false hopes, disillusionment, and disasters. It also brought a decline in both the worldly prestige and the spiritual vigour of Protestantism, especially as expressed through the main historic denominations.

Half-way through the century the view of the world looked very different. The British Empire had gone through decline toward dissolution, although the effects were masked for a time by the Commonwealth idea, which turned out to have little political or economic, far less spiritual, substance to it. Russia had declared itself atheist and persecuted all religions more or less impartially, though its rulers were equally ruthless with secular dissidents and even old comrades. Germany was in the grip after 1933 of Adolf Hitler, a lapsed Catholic from the Bavarian-Austrian borderland. His boundless ambition and evil designs were to give new meaning to Gladstone's Victorian rhetoric about 'the negation of God erected into a system of government'. They were also to have, as incidental by-products, the expulsion of Germans from areas of great historic Protestant importance, the temporary subjugation by Communism of the old 'Central Germany', which was the homeland of Luther, Bach, and Goethe, and a vastly increased political Roman Catholic influence in the West Germany which became the Federal Republic.

In Italy the anti-clerical and ex-Socialist adventurer,

Benito Mussolini, who had come to power was realistic enough to reach a concordat with the Pope, and the Vatican City entered the stamp catalogues of the world. In the United States Woodrow Wilson had given way to isolationism and (as the candidature of Alfred Smith in Wilson's old party suggested in 1928) politics were becoming less dominated by old-style Protestants. The Protestant impulses of Middle America and the Bible Belt had been diverted into the disastrous experiment of prohibition. Statistically there was no great sign of Protestant decline and there were Protestant theologians and church leaders with considerable intellectual influence beyond the theology faculties – Karl Barth, for example, in Germany and Switzerland and Reinhold Niebuhr in the United States and the rest of the English-speaking world. But even where there was vigour in Protestantism it often seemed to reject both established conservatism and traditional liberalism in the Church, as George MacLeod did in Scotland with an Iona Community tinged with pacifism and Socialism rather than the Romanism of which it was at first suspected.

What had gone wrong? The greatest single factor was probably the near-destruction of European civilisation in the First World War and its aftermath (which included a second and even more destructive war) and a reaction against the apparently established and accepted values of the complacent pre-war society. But even now, as the twentieth century draws turbulently to a close, there can be no definitive answers. For one thing not everything did go wrong. Christianity did deepen its roots in Africa and China. It survived persecution in the Soviet Union. The opposition to totalitarianism in its different forms came from eminent saints and obscure ones. In face of Hitler the Christian resistance covered a wide range of political and theological attitudes. Some of those who were martyred for resistance to Hitler were Jesuits and other Roman Catholics but many more were very traditional Protestants, including Prussians. Astonishingly, up to and including George Bush, every American President but one — John F. Kennedy — was drawn from the Protestant denominations. And perhaps the decisive moment in Kennedy's 1960 campaign was his successful bid to persuade enough Protestants to exclude the religious factor from the campaign.

Even in Britain, which seemed to have gone agnostic, a disproportionate number of political leaders — even such arch-enemies as Margaret Thatcher and Edward Heath — were drawn from the diminished ranks of committed and not merely nominal Christians.

What most clearly went wrong was the failure of progress. The nineteenth century (once Napoleon was safely deported to St Helena) was a happier century in many respects than the twentieth, once ludicrously described as 'the century of the common man'.

And the most conspicuous failures of progress were the First World War and its aftermath, which not only made the Second World War inevitable but created diabolical régimes and ideologies capable of killing millions of people in cold blood. What in 1900 had seemed the great strength of Protestantism, and especially of liberal Protestantism, turned out to be its weakness. It had appealed to reason. It had preached progress, if not perfectability. It had lost its fanaticism and even ceased to understand fanaticism in other people.

These weaknesses were not fatal. In so far as they still apply, they are not necessarily crippling. Arguably, it was not the idea of progress but the naivety with which the idea was held, in face of much evidence to the contrary, that was so disastrous — not only before 1914 but after 1945.

How else can one explain, for example, the way that Christians of intellectual and moral substance, such as the Czech theologian Josef Hromadka, collaborated with Communism? Something 'progressive' was thought to lurk amid the evil, cruelty, arrogance, and oppression. An unbiblical view of historical inevitability — a Marxist distortion of Christian eschatological thinking — had blinded much of a mid-century generation not only to a profounder revelation but to the God-given exercise of true reason. It was never truly rational to believe in Marxism any more than it was rational to accept the myths of Hitler's National Socialism, or for that matter the absurd expectations of the French Revolution about the universal and harmonious spread of liberty, equality, and fraternity. It should be possible to guard against these and similar errors by seeking a truly biblical understanding of the nature and destiny of humanity and of the God who has shaped both the nature and the destiny: what the catechism calls the chief end of man.

There was almost exactly a century between the end of the French Revolutionary wars at Waterloo (for Napoleon Bonaparte was a creature and product of the revolution) and the outbreak of the First World War in 1914. It was the Protestant century. But it was to be followed by the lost century — lost partly because Protestantism lost its way by underestimating the force of evil, the power of sin, and the need for Grace, to which human reason must always be subordinated.

But end-of-twentieth-century Protestantism can learn from the achievements of the Victorians as well as the disasters which befell their successors. In the century from Waterloo to Sarajevo, Protestant values — Victorian values if you like — were by no means universally accepted or triumphant but they tended to set the agenda. The dominant patterns of economic and political development reflected the experience and success of Protestant societies. A liberalism which had evolved in Protestant soil was transplanted, with indifferent success to the different climate of Spain or Italy. Protestant concepts of education − as expressed by such different Christians as Thomas Babington Macaulay and Alexander Duff − changed the face of India as much as the East India Company or imperial rule did. American influence transformed Japan (though only in material ways) and penetrated China. The British world dominance created by industrial and sea power established a group of self-governing colonies which reflected the cultures of the British Isles and Northern Europe. The United States − once it survived what was not just an American but a Protestant civil war − began to develop its resources, hinterland, and internal market in ways which made clear that it would eventually overtake the other English-speaking power.

Most of what has been worthwhile in the twentieth century has built on these achievements. As our century draws to a close many of them are being re-evaluated and others rediscovered, not least the capacity for a free market economy to co-exist with a social conscience.

As this is written the Soviet Union seems to be moving away from its cruel and disastrous Marxist-Leninist experiment, though it remains divided and hesitant about which direction to take. Germany, though without its old Eastern provinces, has recovered its unity. Europe, emerging both from its divisions and its old imperialisms, may find a unity it has scarcely known since the break-up of the Roman empire which was preserved after a fashion in the Latin and Greek divisions of medieval Christendom. The United States, though under cultural pressures from a new wave of

Hispanic immigration, has at last tackled (as far as it can be tackled by law) the task that was bungled after 1865, when the former slaves were enlisted in an attempt to subjugate the defeated South, only to be frustrated by a new alliance of Northern and Southern whites reflecting the racial attitudes of the time. Now that the South has accepted equality in civil rights, its race relations may be happier than those of the North.

In many parts of the world the twenty-first century may have an obvious opportunity to learn from the failures of the twentieth, even in some things to make a new and chastened start. But there can be no reversion to the cultural assumptions of the past. The majority of the world's population has learned new myths about imperialism and anti-colonialism as powerful as those of 'the white man's burden'. Even the economic triumph of the United States and Western Europe over the rival Soviet system is qualified by the Japanese demonstration that an Asian and non-Christian culture can contrive capitalist success as dramatic as anything inspired by the Protestant ethic.

There is much that can never be the same again, including something even more important than that 'Protestant ethic' of hard work, honesty, and prudence — the deeper ethos of Protestantism.

After the lost century, Protestantism faces the new century divided and uncertain, lacking in self-confidence and in many countries of its old heartland in statistical as well as moral decline — either in simple numerical terms or in its relative influence in cultural, intellectual, and political life. The pattern of European development seems to have been set by the immediate post-war alliance of the three Roman Catholic politicians in France, Germany, and Italy — Robert Schuman, Konrad Adenauer, and Alcide de Gasperi, though French and German Protestants also had considerable influence in shaping the European Economic Community. A Polish Pope had a very significant influence in challenging Communist power, though perhaps the neo-Orthodox Solzhenitsyn was even more the Luther who nailed the theses of truth to the door that was closed to freedom. Parts of Protestantism have been confused or even discredited by collaboration with Communism, while those leaders or ordinary people who have emerged creditably or even at times heroically (like Laszlo Tökes or such Soviet Protestant dissidents as Georgi Vins) have seemed to have a marginal role.

Even in East Germany the Church seemed, although uncorrupted, to respond to the popular demand rather than to shape it. In the United States the most evangelical of a modern succession of Protestant presidents, Jimmy Carter, was by far the least effective while the most positively Protestant of British Prime Ministers, Margaret Thatcher, had for most of her term been constantly harassed and criticised by the politically-minded leadership of the main Protestant Churches. And while a proportion of Third World leaders have been believing Protestant Christians, their political role and style has hardly differed from that of mission-school former pupils, whether of Scots or Jesuits, who have created secular or even Marxist facades for their power-structures.

But complexity need not mean hopeless confusion. To abandon hope is to renounce belief. The rest of this book is devoted to an analysis and argument suggesting that Protestantism has greater intrinsic strength, external influence, and future potential than is immediately apparent in the modern world. It deserves to be taken far more seriously by people of other faiths and none, and by the other sectors of

Christianity. It also needs in its internal self-analysis and its private quarrels to apply the Gamaliel test — see Acts 5 — to its own hopes, fears, and fond illusions. The things that are of purely human construction will come to nothing. They are bound to fail. What is of God, from God, for God cannot be overthrown.

7

THE CASE OF THE KIRK

If anyone can't stand Scots or Scotland they could skip this chapter. But they would be missing something. There is a need at times to look at the particular without being parochial. To do so can put general theories to the test. But comparisons and evidence from farther afield can also help to lighten some local darkness, even lift some clouds of depression.

I have placed this chapter between the end of a mainly historical survey and a move into the area of dilemmas and Protestant opportunities. That is partly to make it easier for those so minded to skip it most conveniently. It is also because Scottish Presbyterianism (most of it now encompassed in the Church of Scotland, popularly and journalistically known as the Kirk) often seems to be trapped between a proud and turbulent history and a very uncertain future. It is very conscious of its dilemmas, inclined to fits of depression, and far from agreed about where its opportunities lie.

Of course I also pause to look at the Kirk's condition in some detail because this is the area and dilemma of Protestant Christendom that I know best. I worked within it for eighteen years as the editor of its principal journal and have seen Scots Presbyterianism from the very different perspectives of a back gallery pew, a Kirk Session of almost Congregational independence, and what is sometimes wrongly described as the Edinburgh Vatican or the headquarters of the Kirk. It can't be either, for the headquarters of the Church of Scotland are in Heaven.

For the Kirk's sake – which only matters if it means for Christ's sake – I wrote authorised versions of the lives and hopes of innumerable Moderators, suffered a fair amount of folly gladly, and even found myself shaking a limp hand with a rather tired and slightly bemused looking Pope during his Scottish visit in 1982. I think my presence at that strange encounter in the Edinburgh New College quadrangle, beside the statue of John Knox, came about because we had a principal Clerk of Assembly who was Presbyterian enough to insist on at least a few token elders even on so clerical an occasion.

More important than these personal credentials, I think, are those of the Kirk or Church of Scotland, Reformed in doctrine and Presbyterian in Church government. As its legal constitution declares, it is a 'Church of the Reformation', yet part of the universal or catholic Church and conscious of being in historic continuity (or apostolic succession, if you care for the phrase) with the Church of Ninian and Columba as well as of John Knox and the Covenanters. It is a Church that has set its mark on a nation, for its faults, mistakes, virtues, and achievements are all ineradicably etched on Scottish history. It is also a Church which, partly because of the successful political union with England of 1707, expressed Scottish nationality in a unique way. But it is a Church with a glorious past, a troubled present, and a very uncertain future.

There have been earlier occasions when it seemed to provide either a test-bed or a test case for distinctive styles and problems of Reformed Protestantism. In the seventeenth century it sought to create a godly, reformed commonwealth on a far larger scale than Calvin's city-state of Geneva. In the nineteenth century other Protestant Churches took a keen interest in its great internal quarrel over spiritual independence and State interference which culminated in the split of 1843 known in Scottish history as 'The Disruption', led by Thomas Chalmers, recognised at the time as one of the greatest intellects of Christendom. In our own century most of the Presbyterians reunited on a formula which seemed, even to many Anglicans, to suggest how a free Church could still retain elements of establishment and recognise the principle of a national recognition of religion. In the nineteenth century it had also been a very significant international missionary Church and in the formative years of the ecumenical movement in the earlier part of the twentieth century the Scots Kirk burned bright with enthusiasm and took a pioneer role.

Today it is certainly in statistical decline and often in spiritual uncertainty. Although two-thirds of the Scottish people may declare themselves in surveys to be Presbyterian as well as Protestant, the communicant membership of the Kirk has fallen in a generation (between 1960 and 1990) from 1,300,000 to 800,000 or from about a full third of the adult population to about a fifth. Some crude surveys of denominational allegiance, comparing like with unlike, may even suggest that there are more Roman Catholics in Scotland than actual Kirk communicant members. But, even though it is impossible to compare estimated Roman Catholic population with the quite different statistics of Presbyterian communicant membership, there are other statistics which confirm the widespread perception of the Kirk as ageing and shrinking.

There are the Kirk's own statistics of admission by profession of faith, sometimes called confirmation but traditionally involving slightly older age groups than the Anglican equivalent, itself a shade older than the Lutheran confirmation on the Continent. This has fallen by two-thirds (from nearly 33,000 in 1961 to under 10,000 for the first time in 1988). Even when allowance is made for birth-rate trends the figure makes clear that the main reason for the Kirk's annual loss of between 15,000 and 20,000 members is that recruiting is nowhere like the level needed to replace deaths. These losses are accentuated when for financial reasons churches are closed or united. In theory the displaced members should go elsewhere. In practice many are never seen again. Again, the Kirk's own statistics show that the diminished membership is no more committed than the larger one of a generation ago. Only about 60 per cent of the members on the roll are recorded as actually attending at least one Communion service in a given year.

The last attempt at a census of Scottish Church attendance (published in 1985 by the National Bible Society of Scotland based on 1984 information) estimated an all-age Kirk attendance on a typical Sunday at 361,000, just ahead of an Roman Catholic figure based on less complete returns. These figures, valid as a guide to trends although suspect in some details, also suggested about 145,000 attenders at other Protestant churches.

To outsiders this depressing but accurate summary of the Kirk's position may suggest a moribund Church. But this is far from being the case. If anything the Kirk is hyper-active. It has its quota of charismatics and its enthusiasts for every fad and fashion. It has a growing proportion of conservative evangelicals in its ministry and its candidates for the ministry. It has many very lively parishes, not all of them evangelical in style or theology. Its innumerable committees are dedicated to innovation and experiment. It has a squad of industrial chaplains, a well-run and lively arts centre so open in its outlook that it omits to mention its Kirk connection in its press releases, a wide range of social work (all of it important and some pioneering), a much praised video-making and TV unit, a team of good parish ministers turned into organisers of evangelism, constant revisions of Sunday School programmes, working parties trying to work up enthusiasm for anti-racism and multicultural education, and a Church and Nation Committee totally in harmony with the anti-Conservative opinions of the majority of Scots voters. There is a diminished but still substantial number of people working with overseas Churches which are also helped in other ways, notably through the welcome and support given to some of their divinity students and young ministers.

There is a trendy supplement to the hymn-book and every few years there is a new attempt to restate the elements of Christian belief in terms acceptable to those who find the Confession of Faith and the historic creeds unsuitable or insufficient. These are generally described as popular statements of faith, but in practice they usually prove unpopular. So, in many ways, does the Westminster Confession of Faith, the Kirk's 'subordinate standard' (under Scripture). Even some theological conservatives criticise it in outspoken terms for its inadequate emphasis on the love of Christ and therefore on Grace. But so far the attempts to replace the Confession or relegate it to some vague status as a historic document have failed, in one case at the last General Assembly hurdle before the change was legally completed.

In practice the theology emphasised in the Kirk is rather different. No ecumenical conference of significance goes unattended — however extravagant the fare, in either sense of the phrase. No public issue of importance, whether Scottish, national, or international is allowed to pass without comment. It all adds up to an impressive mixture of good works diluted by some daft ideas, and yet it profits the Kirk very little. Much of it is worth doing; some of it reaches to the heart of the faith. And all of these centrally organised activities go with the earnest preaching Sunday by Sunday (for the sermon is still the heart of the Presbyterian service) and a high level of pastoral concern, especially in bereavement and hospital visiting. Many ministers, though not all, also try to maintain the tradition of general parish visitation, especially to the homes of Kirk members, as far as the size of modern parishes allows.

Yet the nation often appears as unmoved by these supposedly relevant activities as it would be by a set of Sunday evening sermons on the Apocrypha. More churches close every year. The committees responsible for this planned contraction are proud of their work, or at least convinced that it is necessary. The decline in membership continues. The Kirk gets a good press but itself shows all the symptoms of a popular newspaper with a declining circulation, uncertain how far to risk alienating faithful readers and unsteady in its judgment about how to add to them.

It can be difficult to decide how far the pattern of contraction, in so far as it represents a real spiritual and pastoral decline and not merely a loss on paper, differs from general Western European and North American patterns.

Some of the obvious factors in the Scottish situation reflect a Scots historical inheritance, for example from the nineteenth-century division of Scots Presbyterianism into three major Churches. These earlier divisions meant that the reunited Scots Kirk sometimes had three churches where two or even one might have done. The 1929 settlement also meant that the reunited Scots Church, which had some privileges of an established State Church without State control or interference, had also uneasy compromises. It inherited some weaknesses both of established Churches and of free Churches.

For example it does not have the benefit of any State-organised optional church tax to which nominal members may still contribute. Until grants for historic buildings recently became more accessible it did not have help from the State (except in one or two cases) in maintaining its inheritance in stone. Its rites of initiation for new members varied (and still vary) from one place to another and among different strands in the Presbyterian tradition. They fall between the Lutheran style of confirmation which is a social rite as well as a religious one and the intense earnestness accompanying 'believers' baptism' or profession of faith as practised in smaller denominations. In a body as comprehensive as the Church of Scotland equivalents of both patterns can be found but most congregations fall somewhere in between. The result is that the Kirk has lost, in face of increasing secularisation in society, much of the nominal adherence that came from social custom. Yet it has not had a strong enough evangelical base to ensure that a numerically diminished Church could strengthen its influence through quality of Christian testimony.

It is also a fact of Scottish life that the Kirk's still considerable influence is very unevenly spread. Too much is often made of the supposed alienation of the working classes in the last century. Arguably these old slogans, linked to half-truths, superficial sociology, and a good deal of political Socialism on the left of the Kirk, have diverted attention from two significant trends. The first is the loss of working-class support, not in the last century but since the Second World War. The second is a dangerous drift away from the Church in the middle classes, the result not of hostility but of indifference. There are trends, even in Scotland, making society more bourgeois and less proletarian but they are not helping a Church which worries about being too middle-class. There are also marked geographical differences in continuing adherence to the Kirk among the Protestant population, at least as far as actual church attendance goes. The 1984 church census, when analysed, suggested not only (as one expected) that attendance was very high in the Western Isles but that it varied greatly between, say, industrial Lanarkshire and areas such as Tayside, Fife, and the Lothians where the Kirk looks stronger on paper but perhaps isn't.

Sociology is not all bunk. The image of the Kirk is a middle-class one. There are attitudes that 'the Kirk's no' for the likes o'us'. But at the other end of the social scale there is a tendency — the strength of which varies between different parts of Scotland — for it not to be for the lairds and gentry either, thanks to the survival of old Episcopalian traditions and the later influence of English public-school education. The peerage and the proletariat are both under-represented in the Kirk compared to the lawyers, the bank managers, the shopkeepers, and the doctors. A generation ago one would have added 'and the teachers', but this may be less marked today. There has probably also been a loss in the numbers of skilled workmen found both in the pews and in the eldership, though a large proportion of today's middle-class and professional members of the Kirk are probably sons and daughters of these people, with their intense passion for self-respect and self-improvement. They created a moral and intellectual climate in which their children could hardly fail to take advantage of widening educational opportunities.

But the Kirk's problems are wider than these. With all its faults it draws strength and support from every section of Scottish society, even if the mix is a bit uneven. Some problems may be common to all Western Christianity, not just Protestantism, but some may be special difficulties of Reformed Protestantism.

For example, there is the emphasis on the preaching of the Word in a way which deserves intellectual respect and demands intellectual response. This is not the style of communication most suited to the fashions of our time, which takes the spoken word in sound-bites rather than solid portions and is happier anyway with the visual image. There is also the emphasis on the written Word in an age when some people leave school with reading difficulties and many more are used only to popular newspapers with more pictures than solid type. Yet the Reformed Faith demands that the Word be read and responded to.

The problem is eased but not solved by the use of modern translations, even some which carry simplification almost to the point of paraphrasing. It remains when the thoughts and the original language are complex as well as profound – for example in Romans 8 or even the opening chapter of John's Gospel. The thoughts as well as the words are far from the level of the people's popular reading and TV viewing.

Important though these factors are, however, they do not

go to the heart of the Church of Scotland's difficulty. Calvinism, even in the relatively diluted form in which most Scots Presbyterians have known it in the last century, is an intellectually and morally demanding form of Christianity, perhaps the most demanding. It expects a sense of vocation in daily life to match that which in other Christian variants is exacted of monks and nuns under special vows and regulations. It demands of the individual what the monastic team spirit tries to provide. Many of us are simply not up to it, though we may try to make something of it with God's grace, however dimly understood, and with some residual support from the moral and spiritual capital accumulated by earlier Scottish (or Irish) generations.

But there are parallels in Churches with different styles and even different theologies. For example much that is written about the problems of parish ministry in the Kirk could, with a little change in terminology, apply to those of the Church of England. They may also be found in all the broadly-based 'national' Churches of Western Europe and the larger Protestant denominations of the USA. They have resemblances to situations in the Roman Church, though it has its own marked differences between (say) Ireland and France.

These are perhaps the marks of these troubled Churches:

Membership has fallen without any compensating increase in the average intensity of commitment and practice among those who remain.

Traditional confessions of belief have either been amended or so modified in practice that they have lost meaning and precision. But the new confessional order

73

seems to bring neither doctrinal stability nor durability.

Traditional moral assumptions have also come into question, with consequent pastoral strain and confusion. Protestant Churches have discovered that the ministry is not immune from the strains on marriage, and almost all the Churches in varying degree have been affected by campaigning to have homosexual attitudes and practices made acceptable. The Kirk seems as much affected as any by the strains on ministerial marriages, much less affected by the lobbying of male and female homosexual groups.

All these Churches have been influenced by women's liberation and feminist trends, although the strength of this trend in America still takes most Europeans by surprise, for example when 'inclusive language' is suggested. But the Kirk has got off lightly so far, especially compared to the Church of England — probably because it accepted the ordination of women in the 1960's. Most of its feminism has been rational and persuasive rather than aggressive and strident.

Most of these Churches are worried about being too middle-class. Those doing the worrying are themselves usually very obviously middle-class. But this subjective anxiety does go with objective evidence that the Church draws disproportionately for leadership and membership on some sections of society.

And almost all these Churches — with exceptions like the Irish Presbyterians — have tended to redefine mission in sociological and even semi-political terms rather than evangelical ones. Almost all developed powerful pacifist and especially anti-nuclear lobbies during the Cold War. Most were so fixed on Third World and anti-apartheid concerns that they were taken by surprise and even taken aback at the swiftness of the East European revolutions in 1989. Most now show signs of diverting this political concern into ecological enthusiasms.

I have deliberately offered this much summarised general theory before trying to identify further characteristics of the Kirk in particular. The Scots Kirk likes to think of itself as being very distinctive, as in some ways it is. But in some things it is not distinctive enough and suffers from all too many general ills of the Western Church. But it does have additional problems. Not only does it get the worst of both worlds in trying to be established and free at the same time; it also contrives to combine the worst effects of international ecumenical influence and susceptibility to the milder forms of Scottish nationalism.

Here I well know I am moving beyond analysis into opinion, and fairly strong opinion at that. I do so partly to encourage those in the congregations (and there are many) who have felt that something was getting out of balance but found it hard to say exactly what. But I want to provoke those who accept that there may be some truth in this thesis to say how much and where it lies. I also hope to reach, however ineffectively, those who in their ideas reflect the prevailing mood in the Kirk. I sum it up as combining defeatism, complacency, and concern for secular relevance. Some of those who express it seem to me much too susceptible to flattery from people who have no time for the Church (or more important, for the things of God) but who are happy to have the Kirk as an ally in their secular causes.

At the very least I hope those who instinctively disagree with me will take into account arguments which are unfashionable in modern Scotland about the chief end of man, and that they will at least appreciate that there are dangers when all men in some very political quarters speak well of them. In any event success in a Christian disputation – perhaps in any argument – does not lie in trying to crush one's opponents and it is not measured by votes. It may consist merely in inducing someone to say: 'I never thought of it that way before.'

It is in that spirit that I set out three propositions where I see self-defeating, even self-destructive tendencies at work in the Kirk. It has allowed its national character to take precedence over the Reformed character it has had since the sixteenth century. It has failed to solve the problems of tolerance and comprehensiveness which are more acute in a national Church than in a denomination. And too often it has shown itself unwilling to seek and find a distinctively Protestant witness in a style appropriate in tone and substance to the new climate associated with Pope John XXIII.

There are times when it is appropriate for the Kirk to emphasise what is distinctively Scottish about it, as well as to ensure that it has an adequate interchange of ideas with other national Churches such as those of England and the Scandinavian countries. There is a similarity of pastoral situation and missionary opportunity linked to a place in community life. But there are times when the Kirk's sense of being a national Church wanders off in quite different directions. Sometimes they are political, stopping short of the line currently favoured by the Scottish National Party – 'independence in Europe' – but appealing to the same emotions. In theory the consistent majority position of the

General Assembly is support for some kind of self-government within the United Kingdom, though the Church and Nation Committee of the day was sharply rapped by the Commission of the General Assembly when it appeared to be calling for a 'Yes' vote in the 1979 devolution referendum. In practice this has never developed into reasoned argument for limited devolution of limited government. Instead (especially during Mrs Thatcher's Premiership between 1979 and 1990) it consisted largely of calls for interventionist policies in economics and social welfare, but with the interventions organised from Edinburgh rather than London.

There are arguments for such policies. But are they arguments which are at all related to the view of man's chief end set out in the Bible, or to the nature of the Church and its role of the 'gathering and perfecting of the saints in this life'?

That some of Scotland's best Protestant and Reformed Christians believe passionately in independence for Scotland, and others for a large but lesser form of self- government, I do not doubt. But is it, in a free society, the role of the Church to be so deeply involved in politics?

There is, however, a significant factor to be taken into account, one which the most zealous unionist would have to accept as an extenuating circumstance and which explains some of the Kirk's problems without solving them. From the Act of Union of 1707 until the rise of modern Scottish nationalism — itself a reaction to an extension of the role of government far beyond anything dreamed of in 1707 — the Kirk and its Presbyterianism were for most Scots a focus of national identity within the United Kingdom. It affirmed an important difference from the English, and it made possible a remarkable degree of self-government not only in the established form of Christianity but in the universities, schools, and social services — for the Kirk was Scotland's Ministry of Education and Social Welfare.

The system stood up well to the increased role of secular Government in the nineteenth century, though it came under strain once industrial changes weakened the old Scots enthusiasm (shared by such titans of the Church as Thomas Chalmers as well as by Adam Smith) for a free market economy. A far greater strain was inevitable as soon as a majority of Scots either adhered to non-Presbyterian Christianity or were only nominally Protestant or were indifferent to religion altogether. The Kirk cannot express any identity for such a Scottish majority. It can only find its own identity if it has a strong sense of its Reformed character and of much wider Protestant affinities within the universal or catholic Church.

Today's Kirk has to redefine what it means by thinking of itself as the national Church. The term has some meaning not only in history but in the range of pastoral service the Kirk still offers and in the territorial responsibility it accepts for maintaining a parish ministry for every community in Scotland. But such a 'national' Church almost inevitably finds that its contains very diverse forms of Christianity within it. To take one very basic and not at all controversial example: many people who belong to congregations of the Kirk, especially in remote or country areas but even in urban areas with a strong link between church and community, may not think of themselves as Presbyterians. If they moved elsewhere they might revert to being Anglicans or Baptists or Methodists or whatever. Some might even return to Roman Catholic worship. They adhere because they find the local kirk a community church, or because it may be the only church for miles.

That causes no major problem, brings the many talents into the Kirk, and meets a need. The real problem of comprehensiveness arises from the range of theology and practice which can exist in a Reformed Church whose territorial roots may be stronger than its doctrinal convictions.

Much of the diversity is tolerable and even welcome. In a society whose cultural diversity can be discovered instantly by turning the tuning-knob of a radio or glancing at a news-stand it is probably desirable that styles of worship should differ, whether in the music used, the biblical translation read, or the language of the sermon. There may be need for more diversity, especially in areas where a Gospel hall seems closer to the people than the parish kirk.

It is a different matter when the diversity sometimes seems to divide the Kirk more profoundly than denominations are divided and when Presbyterians argue with each other in tones that most Christians would regard as intemperate and inappropriate for arguments with militant atheists. It is also an important matter giving cause for future concern when one school of thought dominates the universities and therefore education for the ministry and a high and possibly increasing proportion of candidates for the ministry comes from the other and evangelical wing of the Church. As some of the issues involved are symptoms in the Kirk of much wider divisions in Protestantism (for example over women's ordination and ecumenism) I look at them elsewhere rather than here. But the Kirk cannot be understood today unless the observer is aware of some of the tensions of a Church in which the liberals are dominant but apprehensive for the future and evangelicals sometimes seem in danger of becoming a Church within the Church. It would be no bad thing if the liberal grip were weakened, but not all the problems come from one side. There have already been problems where evangelical zeal for the Gospel has been only too obviously unseasoned by any Christian tact or humility, for example where ministers who may be very sound about the Great Pope in Rome have seemed to act as little popes in their own parishes.

The ecumenical movement is in itself probably no longer a major cause of tension in the Kirk. Ironically, one of the reasons for this is that the main thrust of ecumenism has moved towards co-operation with the Roman Catholic Church — for example in the creation of the Action of Churches Together in Scotland movement. Such co-operation has to be within limits acceptable to Rome and it sets aside (at least for the near future) the pressures for 'organic unity' which in practice meant that a minority — probably even a minority of the ecumenically minded in the Kirk, but powerfully placed — tried to force bishops into the system and on to an unwilling Church. For nearly thirty years ecumenism in Scotland insisted on going up this blind alley, refusing to take for an answer the No which clearly came when Presbytery and congregational opinion was consulted. Kirk committees have an art of making No sound like Maybe but for the moment the bid to intrude bishops or superintendents has been, if not abandoned, at least suspended. At some stage it may be renewed if the World Council of Churches follows up the *Baptism, Eucharist, and Ministry* report with its hankering after the 'threefold ministry' and its weakness on lay participation in the rule of the Church.

The real contribution of the ecumenical movement to the Kirk's problems is a much less straightforward one. In its early days it emerged naturally from that sense of world-wide Protestant affinity which marked the Victorian age, and it probably reinforced these affinities. But as it widened to include the Orthodox, found increasing opportunity to co-operate with Rome, and reflected the Anglican approach on faith and order matters, it contributed to the most obvious of the modern Kirk's inhibitions. It may still know what it means to be Protestant but is not sure how or when to say it.

A sense of that problem is one of the reasons for this book. I do not think the Kirk has lost its convictions but it has often lost its tongue and occasionally its courage. It was officially tongue-tied when the Pope elected a seventeenth-century Scottish Jesuit, John Ogilvie, as a saint — exercising a vote which properly belongs only to God. It welcomed the Pope — as it should have done — but was less forthright about awkward topics than the Scandinavians were when he ventured there. It did not contrast the public relations of the Pope's words about pilgrimage hand in hand with the reality of the Roman Church's very authoritarian line in Scotland on mixed marriages and its divisive school system. There is a stark contrast between the reticence on some of these matters and the gusto with which some liberal and ecumenical Kirk ministers launch their verbal assaults on the other wing of their own Church.

Nor have those in the Kirk who enthuse about the relation of religion and politics shown much spirit of inquiry into some of these relations at a practical level in the West of Scotland. Why does it appear that the majority of councillors in Glasgow and in its ruling Labour group — perhaps a big majority if the lapsed are included — are drawn from the large Roman Catholic minority of the population? The last five Lord Provosts of Glasgow have been reported to be Roman Catholics. That some of these past and prospective civic heads have been exceptionally able people should not prevent relevant questions being asked in a temperate and rational spirit about some of the processes of participation in local politics. Perhaps this mention of the matter will improve the prospects for a token Protestant at the next vacancy.

No-one wants the Kirk to sound like Ian Paisley with a Glasgow accent. What it needs is not a tribal Protestant assertiveness in the West of Scotland, though far too many ministers enjoy being rude to and about Orangemen rather than giving them a lead in preaching Protestant truth with charity and courtesy, but a sense of worldwide Protestant identity within the wider catholic or universal Church. That is wholly consistent with good relations with Roman Catholics and even co-operation on mutually acceptable terms with the Roman Church authorities as far as their rules allow. It is wrong that the Church of Knox, Melville, Chalmers, and George MacLeod should so often seem hesitant and uncertain about how to proclaim its Christianity through its Protestant character. And to speak more plainly on these matters — always speaking the truth in love — might help the Kirk to find the right mood, tone, and prophetic words on other matters too.

8

LOOKING EAST IN SOLIDARITY

Now it is time to pick up those readers who took things easy while the others opted for the excursion in the last chapter through the misty bens and glens of the Scottish Kirk. More important, it is time to switch the emphasis from history and difficulty to opportunities, some of them unprecedented and often unimaginable only a year or two ago.

It was as some of these changes were unfolding in one East Central European country, Hungary, that a Budapest minister moved and embarrassed me when he meant to be complimentary, flattering, and just a little envious. He admired Scotland, he said, 'I think it is the only country with a Reformed majority.'

Theologically he was drawing a distinction between the Calvinist Reformed or Presbyterian tradition and the other Protestant ones – Lutheran, or Anglican, or Methodist. But something in his voice expressed a sense – understandable and inevitable given the course of his country's history – that the Protestant Church in Hungary was emerging from one kind of pressure to encounter another. Forty years of Communism had isolated it from the mainstream of political, cultural, and social life, yet had so controlled and conditioned it that the revival and recovery of Hungarian freedom seemed largely a secular affair. And if democracy did work and create a new Hungary-in-Europe it seemed inevitable that the most powerful spiritual influence would be the reviving Roman Catholic Church, with its bigger battalions and the prestige of a Polish Pope who had successfully challenged Communism. The Hungarian Protestants (mainly Calvinists or 'Reformed', with some influential Lutherans and vigorous Baptists) were having to adjust to a new freedom in which they were still a minority and in which other forces in their society might have the 'leading role' once claimed by the Communist Party.

Yet, as European Protestant minorities go, the Hungarians are a large and influential one, nominally at least accounting for a quarter of the population and embodying much that is vital in the culture, history, and traditions of their people. Weakened though their own position may have been by the secularisation of Hungarian life under Communism, they are a source of strength and support to far weaker Reformed Churches across their frontiers, mainly with ethnic Hungarians in their membership: at the Slovak end of Czechoslovakia, in the Voivodina region of Yugoslavia, in the Carpathian Ukraine of the Soviet Union just across the Hungarian border; and in Romania, where there are 800,000 Calvinists in Transylvania and the borderlands that were once Hungarian. These minorities have all been doubly suspect to the régimes under which they live, or lived till recently, as Christians in a Communist State dedicated to atheism and as members of cultural groups which cannot share the dominant nationality and nationalism of the territories in which they live. Their situation has much in common with that of many other groups, some of them Protestant, behind what was once the Iron Curtain.

Of course Hungary was never 'Eastern Europe', except in the political sense imposed by the Russian domination after 1945, the suppression of the 1956 revolution, and the imposition of Communist rule until 1989. It belongs to central Europe by geography and its religious culture is Western — Roman Catholic, Calvinist, or Lutheran. But this is where West meets East, with that disputed borderland which often becomes a debatable ground in a more profound sense than is signified merely by the arguments about frontiers and minority rights.

Take Transylvania, for example, a territory rich in Protestant history but where for the most part an ethnic great divide goes with a religious one, for most of the Romanian majority is Orthodox. Only the presence of a 'Greek Catholic' or Uniate minority blurs the picture, as it does in the Western Ukraine and Carpathia: a section of the Eastern Church which under political pressure in past centuries accepted the supremacy of Rome but kept some Orthodox customs in worship and order (for example married parish priests). A different kind of political pressure forced the Uniates back into the Orthodox Church under Communism after the Soviet takeover in the Western Ukraine and Bessarabia and the overthrow of the Romanian monarchy. Only since the 1989 revolutions has a rather confused religious freedom been restored. At the time of writing relations between the Orthodox and the Uniates (and therefore between the Orthodox and Rome) remain distinctly soured and at times and places even embittered. The borderland between Eastern and Western Christendom is still disputed.

In the past Protestantism was largely thought of on this frontier of Eastern Europe, as well as in the solidly Orthodox territory to the East, as a Western European ethnic religion, though the impact of Calvinism on the Magyars was so great (despite the onslaught of the Counter-Reformation) that it was known in some areas as 'the Hungarian religion'. Elsewhere Protestantism was known mainly through Lutheranism, with its obvious German connections, and smaller groups of Baptists and Mennonites, strongly represented among the German settlers encouraged to settle in Russia under the Czars, especially the German-born Catherine the Great.

But the picture was always more complex, and it is important to grasp something of the complexity if we are all to show solidarity with the kaleidoscopic range of Protestantism which is sharing in the liberation and religious revival of Eastern Europe. For example there has been a Reforming foothold in the Slav world since the Czech Hussites paved the way for the success of the Reformation in Bohemia, sustained until both religious freedom and national identity perished at the Battle of the White Mountain outside Prague in 1620. The Czechs, however, are really Westerners speaking a Slav language, and geographically as well as politically the most Western of the Slavs. But there have also been pockets of Protestantism, mainly Lutheran, among the Slovaks further east, for long under Hungarian domination. There is also a tenacious Protestant minority of long standing on the Czechoslovak-Polish border, where Czechs and Poles mingle in the part of Silesia which remained Austrian when the rest became Prussian.

In Poland itself Protestantism was regarded (after its defeat by the Counter-Reformation) as the German religion, and although after the Second World War it seemed likely that the Masurians of East Prussia — a frontier people between the Slav and German worlds — would remain as a substantial Protestant minority in Poland it appears that most of them have now opted to think of themselves as Germans, which meant acceptance in West Germany as immigrants.

Further north along the Baltic coast Protestantism also wore a German face, though after the Russian Revolution (when the Baltic States became independent until Stalin's takeover in 1940) local nationalism affected religious as well as political culture. Beneath the German veneer the Estonians (like their cousins the Finns) had been Lutherans since the Reformation. The Latvians were rather more Protestant than Roman Catholic, while the Lithuanians had (and still have had) small Lutheran and Reformed communities in an overwhelmingly Roman Catholic population. The Baltic States also had smaller Protestant denominations – Methodists and Baptists for example in Estonia. These peoples suffered fearfully under Stalin and his successors, with the mass deportations particularly affecting the articulate and educated groups from which most Protestant Church leadership was drawn. The Churches, Roman Catholic as well as Protestant, were doubly suspect. They were at odds with the atheist basis of the Soviet State and its puppet Baltic Republics and they were a potential focus for nationalist discontent.

Until the late 1980's the Soviet Government contained this problem by a combination of tight controls and imposed Church government. In Latvia and Estonia the Lutheran Churches appeared to be totally conformist and in terminal decline, even after the Lithuanian Roman Catholics began to take heart from events just across the border in Poland. For a time the main signs of vigour were among Baptists, though a revival of Estonian Methodists seems to have begun even before the political situation was transformed in the troubled era of Mr Gorbachev. But there was still life even in those Churches that seemed decayed beyond recovery. The diminished number of congregations appeared to be composed mainly of old women, but, as an Estonian pastor put it to me once he was free to speak and travel: 'We owe a lot to these little old ladies, for they kept the Church alive.' As Communism collapsed as a moral system and ran into both political and economic troubles something happened similar to the revolt of the Calvinist Laszlo Tökes against the tame bishops imposed by the Romanian Government on the Reformed Church: in Latvia the Church leadership (including the archbishop) was displaced by the pastors whom the KGB had been telling it to keep in better order.

Solidarity with these Christians once involved trying to find out what was happening to them, which could mean reading between the lines of official statements, or recognising official lies for what they were, or keeping in touch with dissident opinions or the kind of materials which circulated privately among believers and often reached the West. This is the work which Keston College developed so well. In the new climate of opinion solidarity means following news of what is happening, listening to free opinions from what may be discordant voices, and offering whatever help is asked for and can practicably be sent.

Inevitably contacts among Protestant Churches will to some extent revert to confessional patterns. For example the main source of practical encouragement to the Baltic Lutherans is likely to be from Germany and Scandinavia. Presbyterians are developing the contacts (never broken) in Hungary and Czechoslovakia. Baptists have flourished not only in the Ukraine and Russia but in unexpected places, such as Romania — in their case mainly among ethnic Romanians, not the minorities.

But there is a Protestant factor, and a Protestant future, in the hinterland of the Soviet Union and in China that cries out for a much broader Protestant feeling of solidarity, quite consistent with an even wider ecumenical response to the greatest Christian revival of our time. It would be rash to predict what influence Protestantism will have on countries whose future is uncertain and likely to be disputed. In each of these vast empires quite new and unpredictable situations will develop, with new party and ideological lines of division emerging and probably ethnic tensions of which we know little or nothing.

A year or two ago how many of us knew about the Christian Armenian enclave in Azerbaijan? How many of us today (apart from some old China missionary hands) know about the distinctive peoples on the fringe of the Chinese empire? It is not only in Europe that the cultural expression of religious life is closely linked to linguistic, ethnic, and geographical factors. See for example the way that among the islands of Indonesia (a relatively free country) there are numerous Reformed Churches adding territorial as well as theological variety.

Here and there in that vast continental landscape that stretches across the European steppes into Asia we shall find familiar landmarks. Even though many Russians of German descent want to emigrate to the Federal Republic there will be Lutherans and Mennonites scattered across Siberia in small handfuls, some of them becoming Russianised. In China, through the fog and fuzz and official propaganda, we can see that not all trace of denominational missionary connections has been lost. And of course when Hong Kong is incorporated in China most of the Christians there will remain, with far fresher Western connections that those of the 'Three-Self Movement' and the China Christian

Council.

But Western Protestants must expect to find that evangelical Christianity in this vast and diverse land-mass takes new and native forms. Already there is a problem (as there was even before the Communist takeover in China) of heterodox sects mingling Christian elements with Chinese traditions. As in Africa it may be difficult to define where independency shades off into heresy.

Western Protestants may run into further difficulties in understanding what is happening in the Soviet Union, especially if they encounter one major paradox. At the time of writing it seems likely that the ideas we think of as 'Western' will make further progress in the Soviet Union, though whether words like democracy, liberal, and even market economy will mean the same there as they do in the West remains to be seen. Let there be a cautionary warning in the fact that for more than seventy years the Soviet Union under Communist rule has used a vocabulary drawn from Western political and economic thought. It not only gave its own strange meaning to 'democracy' but it drew its ideological language, including the argot of atheism, from the West. Karl Marx was a lapsed Protestant (though of Jewish descent) and every inch a Westerner.

There also remains a considerable threat to complete religious and other freedom from the powerful old guard and vested interests of the Communist Party, and uncertainty about the quality of leadership in the Churches, especially the Orthodox hierarchy.

But let us be hopeful. The Soviet Union, the Russians as well as the other nationalities, see much in the political and economic ideas of the West that they would like to borrow or naturalise. They want personal and cultural freedom as well as more food and goods. But there is still a paradox.

They will use their freedom to explore their own culture and history, and especially to rediscover their art, literature, and religion – all of it intimately bound up with Christianity. But within that Christian tradition there is a suspicion of the West, partly reflecting the history and theology of Orthodoxy, partly reflecting suspicion of the culture which produced the Jesuits, Napoleon, and Hitler. (I include the Jesuits in that unholy trinity not out of epigrammatic Protestant bigotry but remembering how savage Tolstoy could be about them.)

There probably will be a Roman Catholic revival on the fringes of the Soviet Union – this is already happening in the Western Ukraine (through Rome's Uniate connection) and in Lithuania on a big scale – and conceivably some Russians may find much more to admire in the attitude of Pope John Paul II to Communism than in the convoluted dealings of the Orthodox hierarchy with the State. But there can be little doubt that Christian revival in Russia means the grass-roots revival of Orthodoxy. The Orthodox Christians want back the churches that were stolen from them. They want freedom to revive monastic traditions very different from those of the West. And they are likely to express their faith very often both in doctrines and styles which Protestants find uncongenial and worse. Mariolatry, for example, is no preserve of Rome. Their conservatives in theological and liturgical matters may make the guardians of Roman tradition in the Vatican seem arch-liberals and innovators in comparison. Their more independent thinking will probably owe much to Russians who have been influenced by the West but in many ways have kept their distance: Dostoyevsky, Berdyayev, perhaps Tolstoy, possibly Solzhenitsyn. A good deal of energy will go into producing and popularising a truthful history of the Soviet persecution of the Church and canonising a substantial company of martyrs for the Faith.

It is also possible that the moral and intellectual wilderness left by the failure of Communism may prove good ground for Russian nationalism that seeks to identify with the Orthodox tradition. Not all of those who respond to that appeal will be either as liberal (in the best sense of the word) or as well informed as Solzhenitsyn. 'Holy Russia' may become a slogan and the ceremonies of Orthodoxy the outward and visible symbols of nationality rather than spirituality.

But Protestant solidarity will have to be with all Christians of the Soviet Union, not just with fellow-Protestants. They have all been subjected to so prolonged and profound an ordeal that they all need help and all have much to teach. We shall learn from the way they respond to freedom and relate to the majority of non-believers and half-believers around them. However there ought to be a special solidarity between the Protestant world in the West and the large, mixed, and scattered evangelical communities of the Soviet Union, whatever names they go by.

How numerous they are remains a matter of uncertainty. In his book on *Gorbachev, Glasnost, and the Gospel* Michael Bourdeaux draws attention to one of the stranger consequences of the new freedom and respect for truth in the Soviet Union. The best-known and largest Protestant body, the Baptist Federation known during the years of persecution as 'the official Baptists', has scaled down its membership figure from 500,000 to fewer than 250,000 (though of course this is commited membership of a kind scarcely comparable with the nominal rolls of much larger Churches in the West). He suggests that during the Brezhnev years it may have been State policy to encourage the official body to pitch its claims on the high side. This could have been in order to emphasise its greater numerical importance compared to the unofficial or dissident or 'reform' Baptists who refused to register with the Soviet State because the price of such official recognition and tolerance was an unacceptable control over spiritual matters and denial of many basic religious rights. Moreover Soviet policy was to force all sorts and conditions of evangelicals into the federation in order that they could be more carefully monitored and controlled.

With the new freedom it is likely that small Protestant groups may go their own way and that there will be a significant Pentecostal element in Protestantism separated from the main Baptist group, reinforced though this will be by the adherence of many former 'unofficials'. In practice it appears that the line between conformists and dissidents was never as clearly as drawn as some people in the West thought. This should not surprise us. Something similar happened in Scotland in the seventeenth century when most Presbyterians conformed to an imposed episcopal system under Charles II and a determined minority risked and sometimes suffered martyrdom rather than compromise their consciences. There is also some evidence of a similar situation in China, where the controlled and conformist 'Three-Self Movement' and the independent-minded evangelicals who formed house churches were not wholly separate but overlapping groups of Christians.

We should also keep in mind the possibility that groups outside the mainstream of Protestantism, such as the Seventh Day Adventists, may make substantial progress in the Soviet Union, and in China if conditions allow. Michael Bourdeaux, for example, brings out the way in which this group, hitherto only 'on the fringes of legality', have won praise in the new climate which not only tolerates but encourages Christian social work, citing a case where an orphanage had been saved from chaos by the intervention of a Seventh Day Adventist paediatrician, the help of his congregation, and even their use of the 'Lenin Children's Fund'. Keston College has also made it clear that the Baptists, for all the limitations of their leadership under Brezhnev, have shared with the most vigorous elements in the Orthodox Church in taking the new opportunities now open in hospital and other social work.

Bourdeaux puts the numerical strength of the Baptists, including the former dissidents, at only a hundredth of the Orthodox Church but allows them an importance out of proportion to their numbers, both in their present Soviet and international role and in their potential. Keston has also drawn attention to the new spirit of liveliness and independence which has been seen in various ways within the Baptist ranks, despite the traditional caution of the leadership, not least in the launching of the unofficial journal with the heartening title of *Protestant*.

Western Protestants should beware, however, of assuming that Soviet Protestantism will fit neatly into their own denominational patterns. Apart from the 'ethnic' Churches, such as the Lutherans and the Hungarian-linked Reformed group in Carpathia, the Soviet Protestants have roots in Russian or Ukrainian history. Orthodoxy has not only had its schisms – notably the one which produced the 'Old Believers' – but its dissidents who sought a simpler, more direct, and non-hierarchical community of Christians than so patriarchal and priestly a Church offered. The roots of the Baptist and Pentecostal traditions do not lie only in nineteenth-century Western missions but in the country's own history. They were not so much the results of conversions to Protestantism as of the discovery of it, not with the backing of principalities and powers (as in parts of Europe during the Reformation) but in face of them — more like the Lollards of medieval England or the Vaudois, later 'Waldensians'. Moreover, one of the main 'converting' influences was the example of the German farming immi grants whose life-style and devotion to the Bible aroused the interest of the native Russians.

These foreign connections, past as well as present, could expose some Protestants to criticism and misunderstanding in the new Russia, even if the ferocious anti-religious persecution of the Communist years has gone for ever. When the Orthodox look back beyond 1917 to 'Holy Russia' they find centuries of Christian spirituality and artistic achievement amid the political tyrannies and turmoil. When most Soviet Protestants look back beyond 1917 they see persecution and harassment.

The new Russia will face a major test in discovering whether a revived Orthodoxy can break with a nasty tradition of anti-Semitism, and meet a lesser (but still substantial) test of whether the common Christian experience of witness under pressure, and often persecution, can inspire a new Christian harmony in the post-atheist, post-Communist State, whatever form in may take either in Russia or in the wider area of what is now the Soviet Union. It is a situation which calls for prayer and understanding, and a readiness to accept Christian ways which in things inessential may not be our Western ways.

But by now we should have have learned to adjust to changing patterns of secular power and cultural influence. The whole of Christendom reflects the change in the balance of world power since the end of the age of colonial empires, which were closely identified in different ways and styles with a great age of Christian missions. This is very evident in the affairs of the World Council of Churches, in which the key figures of recent years have not been European or North American but Afro-Caribbean and Latin American. But the change in the balance of influence within Christendom is almost as apparent among more evangelical groups — notably those involved in Lausanne conferences — and in the Roman Church. The liberation of Eastern Europe, complete or partial, adds to the complexity. It may even do something to redress a balance within world Christendom which may have swung too far and too suddenly from Western Europe and North America to Asia, Africa, and South America, and which in the next few decades may affect Roman Catholicism as much as it has affected Protestantism since 1945.

It may be significant that within the Roman Catholic Church the pressures for change which seem to cause most disturbance today are not necessarily those which express the pluralism and liberalism of Western Europe and North America but those much further from Rome itself, especially the radical 'liberation theology' of Latin America. The Roman Church has also its share of troubles in trying to accommodate Christianity to traditional patterns of African life. It seems certain that its power structures will increasingly have to reflect the numerical dominance of Latin America and the sensitivity of Africa. The idea of a black Pope is far less far-fetched than that of a Polish Pope was less than twenty years ago.

Protestants may have mixed feelings about some of these changes. Their instinct is probably to welcome anything which opens the Roman Church to new ideas and breaks up some of its traditional patterns of power. But Latin America seems to be exchanging a theology of superstition for one of secular radicalism; and even the arrival of the Polish Pope with a well-founded aversion to Communism has not always had beneficial results. Karol Wojtyla (otherwise John Paul II) is conspicuously ill at ease with some of the symptoms of Western cultural pluralism and a free market economy. His influence and decided personal views have reinforced much of what conservative and liberal Protestants alike find unwelcome in the Roman Church, from the defence of imposed clerical celibacy to the cults of Our Lord's mother where Polish, Latin American, and Mediterranean folk-religion are conspicuously at odds with Western intellectual trends in Roman Catholic theology as well as with any Bible-based Christianity. The present Pope's bid to uphold Christian values in marriage and towards sex is also well-intentioned rather than especially well-judged or well-informed. Even Catholic Poland is discovering that simplistic Vatican teaching on divorce, clerical celibacy, birth control, and abortion may not meet the needs of a liberated society. The complexities in the Soviet Union are likely to be even greater.

Protestantism, when it is true to itself, offers a Christian view of the nature and destiny of man as exacting and authoritative as any in Roman teaching, yet more flexible in inessentials and far better protected against the human corruption that, with the best of intentions, confuses the interests of ecclesiastical power-structures with the will of God. But it has to think of itself as being universal and 'catholic' in the true sense, which demands an awareness of changing patterns and relationships in the world, and not least within Protestantism itself. That is why what happens in two changing areas where Protestants are very much in a minority — but a potentially influential minority — is so important. One is Eastern Europe, historically dominated by the Orthodox strand in Christianity. The other is the 'Latin' world of Southern Europe and Spanish or Portuguese-speaking America, the traditional reservation of the Roman Church and the area of its greatest missionary triumphs.

9

THE LATIN CONNECTION

Spiritually Protestant Christianity is based on a revelation expressed in Greek and Hebrew, though the most important preaching in that revelation was originally done in Aramaic. But culturally Protestantism reflects its historical strength in Northern Europe and North America, even after its considerable expansion in Africa, Asia, and Australasia. We do not think of Calvin as having a Latin temperament.

Protestantism's future is bound to be shaped by changing world patterns and the forces of growth and decay within the Protestant Churches themselves. The African influence is already evident at any world Church gathering. The Asian influence is less evident but perhaps more complex. For example Britain is more conscious of the historic missionary connection with India than of the impact of the apparently more successful missions in Korea. But in the United States and in many international congregations (including some of Scottish origin) the Korean Christians are making their presence felt. So, for the first time, are the Protestant Latin Americans, for example (on the liberal wing of the Church) Dr. Emilio Castro, general secretary of the World Council of Churches.

Sometimes it is easier to see where changes are at work than where they will lead. Who knows how the 'black' Churches of Caribbean origin and Pentecostal style will affect English Church life in decades ahead? They have already begun to have an impact. Who can say how Christianity will develop in the Soviet Union if the recent political and economic trends continue? Or in Latin America?

This area of great potential used to be regarded as almost closed territory to Protestantism, as it quite literally was for more than three centuries after the Spanish and Portuguese conquest. What was beyond our boundaries may now be our New Frontier. It is not only the Roman Church which may be significantly affected by trends in Latin America.

We think of Latin America as solidly Roman Catholic and Spanish-speaking. It is not. Its largest country – a potential super-power of the distant future – is Portuguese-speaking Brazil. In many countries there are native languages which might at some stage challenge at least the local cultural dominance of Spanish. Moreover there are places where the veneer of Roman Catholic religion as well as of Hispanic culture is fairly thin. Roman Catholic dominance has often been maintained by drawing priests from abroad and by tolerating a popular admixture of traditional and even non-Christian elements with the style of Catholicism imported from Spain and Portugal. And last but not least in the qualifications needed to modify our traditional view of Latin America, there is a substantial Protestant factor.

There are probably four reasons why in Britain we tend to give it relatively little attention. The first is that some of our cultural and economic connections with Latin America were weakened during the two world wars and their aftermath. The second is that the 'Protestant factor' has not until recently been very evident among the dominant social and political groups, except where (as among German-descended Brazilians or Anglo-Argentines) the economic status of some minorities has been divorced from political influence. The third is that Protestantism has been so divided that it is sometimes hard to think of it as a single 'factor' at all. And the fourth is that many of the Protestant groups (and especially the fastest-growing ones) tend to reflect North American rather than European styles of Protestantism and lack the historic missionary connection which in new forms of 'partnership' keep Indian and African Churches relatively close to the main Protestant denominations in the British Isles. We should not exaggerate. Latin America is not on the threshold of a Protestant Reformation. On the other hand we should appreciate that, as in China or India, relatively small percentages of the total population can mean quite large Churches, often with a much higher degree of commitment than the average Church member shows in Britain or Germany.

For example the United Bible Societies (whose world annual report is a valuable record of religious trends and statistics) put the Protestants of Brazil at only 4 per cent of the population, not counting another 2 per cent in non-Roman 'indigenous Churches'. But that 4 per cent amounts to six million people. Less conservative estimates place the figure very much higher. Put it another way: there are probably six times as many Protestants in Brazil as there are in France, where the Protestant minority has always been a signficant force both in national life and world Christianity.

These UBS estimates suggest that, while there are still Latin American countries (Colombia and Cuba for example) where scarcely 1 per cent of the population is

Protestant, the percentage rises in others as high as 12 per cent in parts of Central America (Honduras) and is around 5 per cent in such significant countries as Costa Rica and Guatemala. Even if in most South American countries the proportion of Protestants is no more than 2 or 3 per cent this represents a larger proportion of committed and educated Christians. Given the population growth rate of these countries, it also means that Spanish and Portuguese speakers will become a significant proportion of all Protestant Christians. Immigration trends also mean that in the future a sizeable element of Protestantism in the United States will be of Hispanic origin. The long-term cultural effects of these changes are far from predictable but they will certainly affect the way Protestantism sees itself and is seen by the rest of the world.

There is another 'Latin connection' that the Protestants of North-West Europe also need to foster, even though the Churches involved are very small and unlikely to achieve any spectacular growth or political and cultural impact. Most British visitors to Italy, Spain, and Portugal are probably unaware that there is any indigenous Protestantism there at all. Such indifference is relatively excusable among holidaymakers and Britons working abroad in these countries, since the vast majority of local people they meet will be either practising or nominal Roman Catholics and their own interest in religion (if they have any) will draw them towards expatriate congregations. Unfortunately a less excusable form of blindness can afflict some more exalted visitors. The style and preoccupations of the see of Canterbury (at least until recently) made it unlikely that an archbishop visiting Rome would go out of his way to encourage the Italian Protestants or even notice their existence. It is more surprising to discover that Moderators of the Church of Scotland's General Assembly have been known to visit Rome, even the Vatican, without taking the opportunity to show their solidarity with fellow-Protestants of the Italian Church.

The Waldensian Church in Italy, tiny though it is and still rooted in a few Alpine valleys where it survived persecution, is an older Reformed Church than the Kirk of Scotland. It deserves encouragement, and it has something to offer us. To talk to its pastors is to discover just what ecumenism can mean in practice and to gain an insight into the split personality of the Roman Church today. At the same time in neighbouring dioceses there can be a new spirit and some old and nasty habits. Moreover Christians who belong (as Italian Protestants do) to a culture so deeply imbued with Roman Catholicism can be a great help in distinguishing what is vital in the Protestant expression of Christianity and what is not — not least in attitudes towards the see of Rome.

No Moderator should visit Rome without ensuring that he also visits the Italian Protestants, even though the majority of them (about half a million of all kinds and degrees of commitment) probably now belong to independent groups of Pentecostal inclination. And if he is wise he will also consult them while he is planning his visit. What Rome does at home matters at least as much as what Rome says to the wider world: and not all that it does is discouraging. Waldensians speak of very different attitudes in the Roman Church, varying from place to place and bishop to bishop.

There is a tradition in Scotland of contact with the Italian Protestants, and some individual Anglicans in England and Ireland have maintained the enthusiasm which developed in Victorian times. However English and Irish evangelicals have probably done much more than Scots to maintain and develop the relatively few links between Britain and the small Protestant communities in Spain and Portugal. I admit my own fault in the matter, but it is a pity all the same, for there should be natural affinities between the Scots and the two Iberian countries.

Scots can appreciate better than the English not only the successful assertion of Portuguese nationality but the tensions that exist within Spain between the dominant traditions, attitudes, even accents of the Castilians and the other peoples who are influenced by them and yet react against them. We should understand Catalonia in a way the English never can, and at least the Gaels among us should have a fellow-feeling for the Basques, with their unique minority language and long involvement in the affairs of a much larger country speaking a world language. On a profounder level, there is also a potential affinity between the two styles of Christianity that seem to differ most from each other: the ultra-Calvinist and that high Spanish Catholicism that often seems more papist than the Pope himself, and which seems to have gone a bit out of fashion in the new Spanish democracy and constitutional monarchy.

What a pity it is that Calvinism never had a chance to hold a foothold in Spain, though Protestant exiles had a Bible printed in Basel as early as 1536 and later translated Calvin's Institutes into Spanish. One wonders what it would have made of that emphasis on mortality and the facts of death that gives a special solemnity to the better side of Spanish Catholicism, when the vision of death and eternity reduces to insignficance the whole array of painted dolls in fancy dress that masquerade as images of the Virgin. Only Calvinism could have responded in a positive way to the Jewish traditions of medieval Spain which the Inquisition tried so hard and so cruelly to eradicate.

But who are we to question the ways of Providence? What matters today is that we recognise that evangelicals do exist in both Portugal and Spain. It is especially important not to ignore or forget them because we may find that enlightened elements of the Roman Church display a genuinely ecumenical and Christian spirit. There is nothing new in that. Readers of that great Protestant classic, George Borrow's *The Bible in Spain,* will remember that there were always some priests who would respond to the opportunity to obtain and circulate the Scriptures, and others who could meet a 'heretic' in a welcoming and Christian spirit.

What is new in Spain is the attempt to create not only the forms but the spirit of democracy and constitutional monarchy, including genuine religious freedom. Unfortunately religious freedom in Spain has often meant no more than the chance to be free of religion. Even in the progressive years since the death of Franco not all the changes have been for the better, and the desire to be integrated in Europe has meant imitating a good deal of what has gone wrong with the rest of the continent, from TV game shows to pornography. Hedonism is less troublesome than political and spiritual fanaticism but it is not the chief end of man.

Today Protestants in Spain are able for the first time to take advantage of religious freedom in a temperate political climate. Half a century ago they were caught between two violent forms of extremism, and the Fascist gangs that killed the poet Lorca in Granada also murdered the Protestant pastor there. Yet the 'progressives' who claimed they were fighting for democracy included an anti-Christian element who persecuted, murdered, and burned with a ferocity scarcely known even in the Russian and Chinese Revolutions. And when the civil war ended the handful of Protestants (probably little more than 20,000 and possibly not more than double that today, if expatriates in Spain are not counted) suffered a mixture of profound and petty restrictions under the Franco dictatorship. Now that they are free the Spanish Protestants are not likely to show the spectacular growth of Protestantism in Latin America. But, like the Italian Protestants who have ties with South America, they could provide an important link between the new Latin world and the old one. They will also affirm that there is no culture of human and humane achievement — and the peoples of Cervantes, Camoens, Velasquez, and Goya are rich in cultural inheritance — which does not respond to the Word of God. Rather more of the Protestant future than the Protestant past will be expressed in the elegant tongues of Iberia.

10

PROTESTANT OPPORTUNITIES

Among the major Protestant denominations and many of the smaller ones the last quarter of the twentieth century has proved a time of difficulty and decline. We have been acutely aware of shrinking numbers, lack of commitment among many of those who remain, and financial crises so acute and recurrent that they sometimes divert attention from the far more serious crisis of belief.

We have been blind to some of the successes in the world Church, such as the survival of the Faith under Communist persecution – in spite of and not because of the collaboration of many Church leaders – or the Protestant growth in Latin America. We have drawn the wrong lessons from the vigour of the Church in Africa and have sometimes given it the wrong kind of encouragement.

For example we have given Archbishop Tutu an un-critical acclaim in South African matters, listening to him as eagerly when he pronounces on matters where he speaks with no authority, such as economics and business, as when (as he has done) he stands up for truth and decency in face of violence and hatred. In the Reformed Churches we have shunned our brothers and sisters in some of the

Dutch Reformed Churches, not because of what they do or believe today but because of what they did in the past and what some of them may have believed about a biblical warrant for apartheid. At a time when they most needed our help and understanding, and had made it clear that in Christ there is no black and white any more than there was Greek or Jew in the New Testament, we connived at a tawdry and (as it turned out) disastrous political stunt by electing Dr. Allan Boesak to the presidency of the World Alliance of Reformed Churches, a role for which he was unsuited both in character and temperament.

In the mainstream Churches we have also shown ourselves too supercilious and perhaps a bit envious towards smaller evangelical groups which have been labelled 'fundamentalist', as if their simple and sometimes far too literalist faith was an embarrassment to us and not an encouragement and a challenge.

We are concerned about crises in membership and about money, to which we respond after a fashion. But our greatest crisis is of faith and it is within our Churches and often within ourselves. We don't sound as if we believed in God's power and we act in ways which betray our loss of confidence not only in ourselves but in him.

We are people of little faith. That applies not only to those who admit to doubts — we ought to form ourselves into the Brotherhood of Saint Thomas — but to many of those who preach and practise good works. They tell that we need to go where the people are and listen to what they are saying. But some of those with a deep sense of mission as service can do a disservice to those they are trying to help. We do not tell people about sin, and unless we do we cannot also tell them just how amazing God's grace is. We are in danger of making the good news to the poor sound like a promise to soak the rich.

We concentrate on the inequalities and injustices of Western society in a way that diverts our own attention and other people's from what ought to be the great lesson of our time. Abundance of goods goes too often with spiritual poverty. And at a more intellectual level there is a different kind of failure: an abundance of ideas goes with spiritual famine. Our literature and art often testify not to beauty and love but to a chaos of the spirit, to an angry journey in an aimless quest.

At least in the West, this malaise seems to affect every Christian tradition. But mainstream Protestantism seems to have been particularly vulnerable to it, for reasons that vary between different countries, though a common factor has probably been the overwhelming preponderance of liberal theology and politics among the opinion-formers of the Churches. In the United States liberal Protestantism has historically been the cult of the top people and of 'old money'. In Europe it has also been deeply entrenched, not only in the commercial work ethic from the seventeenth century to the nineteenth but in an ethos of public service, for example in the civil services of Britain, Germany, and France. It is easy to see Protestantism as an inheritance from the past, and perhaps many Protestants, including most of those in Church leadership or influential secular positions, may themselves tend sub-consciously to think of themselves in this way. They have all the characteristics of good trustees, especially caution and probity. They are temperate, restrained, unexcitable, ready to make allowances for thrusting newcomers from less privileged backgrounds.

But other virtues, as well as these, are needed to secure the Protestant future. That means settling the proper future priorities of the Protestant Churches and also appreciating that the future belongs to the ideas of individual freedom and civil liberty inherent in Protestantism. There are opportunities that need to be taken; but they cannot readily be taken if we do not clearly see that they are there for the taking. In some of these matters we need to realise the importance of initiatives that are already being begun, sometimes by parts of the Church whose strength is only to obviously unequal to their task. In other matters too many people simply do not see the opportunities. And in others conservative and liberal Protestants need to agree to differ and to work together.

As an example of under-valued initiatives I instance the response to the potential demand for Bibles in Eastern Europe and China; among opportunities not fully recognised, I suggest the consequences of new thinking in parts of the Roman Church; and of areas where Protestants must show more tolerance of each other, I pick out the often acrimonious wrangles between fundamentalism and liberalism and over the role of women in the leadership of the Church.

Protestantism is positive Christianity and has an evangelical message. Christ died for our sins and is our only mediator with God. The pattern of the visible Church of which, with the invisible Church, he is the only head, is relatively unimportant provided it preaches and teaches the Word and earnestly offers the two Gospel Sacraments, baptism and the Lord's Supper, as means of Grace. It should not modify its teaching to suit a particular ecumenical climate nor seem to be mainly concerned with reacting, positively or adversely, to what is happening in the Roman Church. But what happens there is bound to influence and interest it. The size, the power, the piety, and intellect, as well as the conflict, error, and confusion evident in the

Roman Church will often draw Protestant responses. Both their substance and their mood is important, and they should be inspired by the living Word and Christian experience, which can sometimes take precedence over subordinate standards drafted in other centuries in response to very different conditions.

Whether the papacy is the anti-Christ and whether the Roman Church is a 'synagogue of Satan' seem to me to be unprofitable speculations. To use such terms gives an impression both of bigotry and personal insult. It is far better to advance a proposition which is by no means complimentary to the papacy but which recognises that it is God alone who elects the saints. It is also one tenable with another truth which we ought to recognise, not only when we see believers of all kinds persecuted by atheist régimes, but when we may find a degree of common cause with Roman prelates and the chief rabbi in face of secular assumptions in our own society. We should be guided in three areas by the principle that Roman Catholics are our fellow-Christians, not because of the tenets which are distinctive of their Church but in spite of them. We need to consider how far they share with us the doctrines of the universal or catholic Church. We may often find that there are also pastoral and devotional concerns which we share. And when we consider ceremonies and customs which differ (as they do also between Presbyterians and Pentecostalists or the Salvation Army) we may find that very few of them really involve the substance of the Faith. It is when the Roman Church moves beyond those three areas (for example in exalting the papacy, confusing human power-structures with divine intentions, and setting out unbiblical Marian doctrines) that problems arise for Protestants and especially for those who give weight to their own historic statements of faith — Calvinist, Anglican, or Lutheran. See for example the 1990 reflections of the American Lutherans or the Missouri Synod on the problem of the 'antichrist'.

God surely does not expect us to elevate doctrine above Christian experience, provided such experience does not defy Scripture. He must expect us to read and interpret his Word in the light of our own fallibility and our experience of the gifts and graces of all the saints. Unless we do so, conservative Protestants are likely to be irrelevant spectators when (as is absolutely inevitable) there are further clashes between authority and tradition on one side and conscience and inspiration on the other within the Roman Church, and possiby at some later stage within the Orthodox Churches as they respond to the new cultural conditions of a post-Communist society.

There are great areas, especially in cultivating the spiritual desert left by Communism, where all Christians can work together or at least travel together for some time to come. The most obvious one is the encouragement throughout the world of the renewed interest which in many countries the Roman Catholic Church has shown in the Bible. It is no bigotry to say that the Roman Catholic Church has in places almost reversed its attitude to the spread of the Scriptures and the private use of them in the Christian life. The Orthodox situation is rather different. Only now is it possible in the most important country of the Orthodox tradition to contemplate the widespread circulation of the Bible unhampered either by illiteracy or Communism. Something similar is true of China, though the role of the Bible and the public response to it is likely to be very different. In Russia the Bible is a source-book of national cultural history, as well as of so much else besides. In China it may well appear, to millions and millions who reject

Marxism, as a foreign book expressing alien concepts.

For the moment there is little need for us to differ about the way we read and use the Bible, at least where the Soviet Union and China are concerned. There is still much leeway to make up in providing even Christians with sufficient supplies of Bibles. Many of the signs are promising, despite the slow movement of the Soviet economy towards a free market in which the printing industry there will meet the demand, whether from the Churches or the general population. There are already signs of the emergence of Bible societies and committees, not only in Russia and among the other Slav peoples, or in the Western-looking Baltic States but in Georgia, Armenia, and Moldavia. There are also reports of a 'children's Bible' not only meeting the need for which it was intended but arousing the interest and curiosity of unbelievers whose only acquaintance with the Scriptures is through the ritual denunciations of 'fables' in old-fashioned anti-religious propaganda. If the Orthodox Church succeeds in its efforts to have voluntary extra-curricular classes available in Russian schools this will also immensely stimulate the demand for Bibles. In August 1990 (when the Orthodox Church was trying to have the draft religious law amended to make this kind of religious education explicitly legal) there were already reports of priests and missionaries being able to work in eight Moscow schools.

Politically and intellectually China remained a much more controlled and restricted society even after the Soviet Union began to take real strides towards religious freedom. Yet in China too there were promising signs, partly the result of the earlier economic diversification and relative open-ness to foreigners prepared to work within Chinese rules. For example the Amity Press's successful (if small-scale) printing of Chinese Scriptures in China was ahead of anything achieved in the Soviet Union at that time.

There remain vast uncertainties, especially in China. Christianity, the traditional religion of the Russians and many other Soviet peoples, has proved its survival and capacity for revival whatever direction events in the Soviet Union may take. While survival and capacity to revive have also been proven in China, the situations are so different as to make any comparison misleading. Chinese Christians remain a tiny minority, and if the country were to revert to its pre-Communist traditions we might discover that suspicion of Western religion is one of them.

But there is no doubt that the decline of Communism opens up great opportunities in which Protestants can emphasise the need and duty to make the Bible available to everyone in every tongue, a primary principle of the Reformation. Yet for the foreseeable future they can do so without any risk of major disagreement with Rome and Orthodoxy, at least on this account. We should not exaggerate the likelihood of a vast growth of evangelical Churches, but we should recognise that the future intellectual and religious climate will be much influenced by these 'Protestant' attitudes towards availability of the Bible.

There are certainly areas where many Protestant assumptions will influence future debates within the Roman Church, and indeed where some of the problems which have perplexed Protestants in the earlier part of this century will weaken the authority of that Church over its adherents, whether it maintains the present style of rather heavy-handed papal authority or moves towards a more conciliar and collective leadership. Among them are the untenability of clerical celibacy, the pressure from women for a role in ministry and leadership, the interest in inter-communion, the practical pastoral difficulties of maintaining an unyieldingly hard line on divorce and contraception, the limited appeal of Mariolatry in the better educated sections of the Roman Communion, and the widespread reservation and equivocations among Roman Catholics about the nature of papal authority and the theological and historical arguments which traditionally buttressed it and even steadily increased it until the 1950's.

We need to be realistic. As far as dogma is concerned, and despite the new spirit of ecumenism and the change of many individual attitudes, the aftermath of Vatican Two has not yet even secured the reversal of the disastrous consequences of Vatican One, when the Roman Church (against the resistance and better judgment of many scholars and bishops) was saddled with the doctrine of papal infallibility. This is not only a doctrine irreconcilable with Scripture and unacceptable to Protestants but one as indefensible as it is incomprehensible when explained away by Roman Catholics today who belong to a cultural and intellectual climate utterly different from that of Pius IX in 1870.

A revived, self-confident and tolerably harmonious Protestant sector of Christendom would be well placed to await, encourage, and welcome further changes within the Roman Church. There is the problem. Much of Protestantism remains in decline and lacks self-confidence. And although there is relatively little disharmony between Protestant denominations as such there is a serious, even a destructive disharmony between the wings of Protestantism. That is partly because they have neglected the limited, but still considerable, value of emphasising their common Protestant inheritance as a unifying and restraining factor. It is also because both the liberal and conservative wings of

Protestantism have often allowed their quarrels with each other to count for more than their testimony to the Faith in an age of scepticism and unbelief.

Protestantism now needs within itself at least that degree of restraint, understanding, and charity which marks ecumenical relations between the main Protestant denominations and the post-Vatican II Roman Church. The mutual confession: 'Jesus is Lord!' is certainly quite inadequate as a doctrinal statement but it is a start. Those who call themselves Christians have something in common, and even more so those who assent to the historic or catholic biblically-based doctrines of the Faith. There should be additional factors of unity and understanding, historical and doctrinal, affirmative even in the rejection of error, among the Churches and other groups of Reformation inheritance. To decline assent to the supremacy and infallibility of the papacy is no negative attitude, for no human power-structure has the right to appoint an exclusive Vicar of Christ. To reject such claims is affirmation of the real headship of the Church, as well as a positive reaction to the error-strewn history of the Christian Church.

Sometimes one encounters the view that it doesn't really matter, and that all kinds of checks and balances could be built into the structures of a united Church with papal primacy, together with the right of individual conscience to reject doctrines not of the substance of the Faith, such as the Immaculate Conception, the bodily assumption of the Virgin, the number of sacraments and the Roman view of the Communion of Saints which appears to challenge the role of Christ as the only mediator. And clearly a united Church could not possibily be of one mind on the nature of the Lord's Supper, never mind accept the Council of Trent's view of it.

But of course it does matter. God is truth as well as love. He cannot be adequately honoured in the kind of disagreement such an ecclesiastical empire would have to tolerate. It is difficult enough for a Church to serve him when those who belong to it do so with many doubts and reinterpretations of the statements in its confession or creed. It is still more difficult to construct a Church which takes so many ambiguities into its system.

The same criticism could be made of the mainstream Protestant Churches today. Most of them can be called all things to all men, although the phrase (like so many others from 'brothers in Christ' to 'Son of Man') now needs to be rendered in inclusive language. Yet if they only realise, even their confusion can be turned into a source of strength. For as the wise Pharisee Gamaliel said (see Acts 5) what is of God cannot be overthrown, and much that is of mere human construction will disappear. What they need is to recover the Reformed concept of the invisible Church that coexists with the visible one, superior to it and uncorrupted, yet overlapping with it, even where degeneration has set in and regeneration depends on the grace of God.

It is a grace evident in even the least expected places. The Charles Wesley hymn surely speaks a truth for all God's people everywhere whom he calls to repent. Does it not also apply even to those within the Churches which, with that seventeenth-century flourish and some justification in the events of the time, the confession calls 'synagogues of Satan'?

> His blood can make the foulest clean;
> His blood availed for me.

Theologically, the heart of the Reformation inheritance is

surely justification by faith and the doctrine of Grace. Lutheran, Calvinist, Baptist, and Reformed Anglican need not be separated there. Nor need fundamentalist and liberal. Nor, before the ultimate judgment, need Protestant and Papist or Greek, for whatever is of God in Roman Catholicism or Orthodoxy is there as it is in Protestantism, not by the wisdom of humanity but by the loving kindness and remission of penalties that we call Grace. For that justification is not a distinctively Protestant doctrine but a Christian one, preached by Paul because he found it in Christ, expounded by Augustine of Hippo, and no longer shunned today by Roman Catholic scholars and theologians.

It is not just a matter of saying, as some Christians audibly do in passing round the elements at the Lord's Supper: 'This is for you'. It is Christ's blood that was shed for you, his body broken for you. The bread and wine that represent the flesh and blood are symbols only in their physical substance, though even the Blessed Martin Luther could not quite recognise a metaphor when he met one in the Gospels and the First Epistle to the Corinthians. They are also reminders – 'a memorial of him' – of both God's love and Christ's death, which are inextricably linked in eternity.

They testify too that Christ is really present. However dimly we may sense his presence it becomes more real in the Lord's Supper, not least because we carry out his command in the great company of the Church, visible and invisible, and of time past and time to come as well of the present age.

Yet historically the Lord's Supper, which should unify, has often divided Christians and still seems to keep them apart. But it is not the sacrament of Grace but the human attempt to regulate it, define it, and elaborate it which causes divisions, and which perpetuates even some historic divisions among Protestants. And it was, by the perceptions of the world, not unreasonable in the sixteenth or seventeenth centuries to hope that strict regulation might secure the 'right adminstration' of the sacraments and that with the help of the Holy Spirit a revealed consensus of sacramental doctrine would emerge. More than four centuries later we must sense that the Holy Spirit may lead in a different direction.

The Protestant future cannot be assessed without some consideration of the Lord's Supper, and especially of the role and possibilities of inter-communion.

11

THE LORD'S SUPPER

A few years ago it would have been quite unrealistic, and perhaps also dangerous, to discuss inter-communion, and especially inter-communion involving Rome, in any analysis of the Protestant future. Pressure on Rome to move towards inter-communion came (as largely it still does) from High Anglicans distressed that they regard themselves as 'Catholics' but are not treated as such by the Roman variety. This kind of plea invited Protestant derision as well as Roman rejection, though I have seen it made in very moving terms when the 'pain of division' is not merely a phrase from chattering ecumenists but an expression of hurt. Roman attitudes can certainly create strains in mixed marriages where both partners are genuinely devoted to the faith and the tradition in which they have learned to express it. But conditions, attitudes, and even practices change long before Church law in any denomination may fully recognise the change.

A generation ago Anglicans often seemed as determined to bar unepiscopally confirmed Protestants from the Holy Table in their churches as Romans (or most of them) still are when they decline to welcome such Protestants as might choose to come forward. I remember in the 1950's, in my National Service days, attending a 'moral leadership course' conducted by Church of England chaplains for all denominations who cared to come. But the 'other denominations' were explicitly asked not to come to the Communion service, as it would be embarrassing to have to decline to give them the elements. I never even attended a Communion service in my Oxford college chapel until I went back to a reunion in middle age because I wasn't sure if I was welcome in those distant days, even though our dean was a Rugby-playing Irish Protestant.

I contrast this with the most recent occasion on which I took Communion in the Anglican form, not just because everyone was so obviously welcome, but because it was in a Roman Catholic church. Admittedly, the building is only a shell and the real house of God is the household of the people in it and gathered round the Table; and admittedly it was in Spain, where as in other parts of Europe the Roman Church has become more liberal in the good sense of that term. But could I fail to be grateful for the hospitality (so unthinkable in Franco's day) of those who had lent their church to the heretics and who had gathered round the same Table an hour or two earlier? Could I fail to recognise them as part of the same household of the Faith any more than I could deny solidarity to a recently persecuted Russian Orthodox priest because I deplored his eucharistic theology? More important than these subjective reactions, could any objective analyst of inter-Christian relations − which I hope we can substitute for inter-Church relations − fail to see that such co-operation and good will would inevitably and steadily bring forward both the possibilities and the problems of inter-communion? That is happening today.

In the Church of Scotland the general practice at a Communion service is now to invite those in the congregation who belong to other denominations to join in taking the bread and wine. The Anglican Churches may not have gone so far in theory — I am thinking now of 'ordinary' services and congregations, and not those with a special ecumenical flavour or wider pastoral role — but it has changed its ways in practice and moved irreversibly in the direction of full inter-communion. It is fair to say, even allowing for some Anglican rules and reservations, that inter-communion among the larger Protestant Churches has either been achieved or is in sight.

Rome is another matter, and the problems are not entirely on the one side. While there are undoubtedly Protestants whose consciences have led them to share and even seek Roman Communion on occasions — one Edinburgh minister felt he needed almost daily Communion on a sabbatical term in Assisi, and apparently got in — many Protestant consciences would rebel at the prospect of joining in the Mass. That is quite apart from the problem of members of very conservative denominations who may (as the Lord Chancellor, Lord Mackay of Clashfern found out the hard way) face Church disciplinary proceedings for even being present at a Mass, for example on a requiem occasion. Protestants may very reasonably doubt the propriety of sharing in a ceremony in any way which appears to recognise the special role and powers claimed by Rome for its priests. Nor could they in good conscience — so it appears to me — join in a ceremony which seemed to proclaim the aspects of the Mass which the Thirty-nine Articles of the Church of England called 'blasphemous fables' and the Westminster Confession 'abominably injurious to Christ's one only sacrifice'. That is even without taking into account any lingering flavour of the grosser notions of transubstantiation of the elements.

Yet a degree of inter-communion now exists, however limited, precarious, and informal, between Protestants and Roman Catholics. It is realistic, given the trend of the times and the mood of those involved, to expect it to be extended. Sometimes it appears to involve a stretching and bending of the rules on the Roman side and an assertion on both sides of the right of private judgment. Those involved might say they occasionally set the compulsion of Christian conscience above the rules and regulations of Church structures.

For example at the Protestant service in Worms in 1983 commemorating the 500th anniversary of Martin Luther's birth I discovered that not all the Roman Catholics present had followed the example of their official representatives, who sat quietly while the rest of us rose to be served with bread and wine. I am assured on good authority that something similar happens at the Communion service in the parish church at Whitekirk in East Lothian during the annual ecumenical pilgrimage there.

I was also aware when editing the Church of Scotland's magazine, long before some ministers discussed at the 1990 General Assembly their experience at Roman Catholic Communion services, that some of the leaders of the Kirk whom I most respected had taken the elements at the hands of Roman priests. These were not the people in the Kirk (of whom there are a few) who have lost their inheritance. One has been a magnificent thorn in the flabby flesh of schemes for organic unity based on bishops, as sound on ecumenical matters as I fear he is unsound on political ones. Another is a truly great theologian with a conservative but comprehensive sense of Reformed Christianity as both blessed inheritance and living faith.

For what it is worth, there will also be some public pressures, though these are likely to come more from ecumenical, liberal, and even radical elements in Presbyterianism. For example the Iona Community says it is dedicating itself to seeking inter-communion by the end of the century, and in this field I think it is a force to be reckoned with, thanks to its contacts with liberal elements in the Roman Church. I am not myself a great admirer of the Iona Community, and regard its political influence in the Church of Scotland as wholly pernicious. I also thought it made a great mistake after the Pope's visit to Britain in taking up his slogans – for example about proceeding 'hand in hand' – without challenging him on such practical matters as oppressive and unfair rules on mixed marriages, encouragement of sectarianism in education, and inter-communion. But I do not doubt that the Iona Community (which assures me indignantly that it sees itself as part of the Church of Scotland) proceeds on assumptions which are at the moment totally unacceptable to Rome, though not by any means to all Roman Catholics: first, that (for what such a concept is worth) the ministerial orders of Protestants are no less valid than those of Rome; and secondly that progress to inter-communion must be by mutual acceptance, recognition, and participation. It cannot be a matter of getting some special dispensation to allow Protestants on licence to accept a wafer at the hands of a Roman priest and on his terms. I am sure that the inter-communion the Iona people hope for is through universal acceptance that the Lord Jesus Christ is the unseen president at every Communion Table.

Despite these signs of important changes that have happened already, and of others that will at least have to be discussed, there is not likely to be any dramatic break-through. The limitation of the Iona tactics is that they concentrate attention on what Church authorities say and do in public, and possibly create difficulties for people who might do much more remarkable things in obscure but significant settings. Pressure on Rome over inter-communion puts its Church authorities in embarrassing positions, forced to sacrifice their public image of sweet-ness and ecumenical light rather than surrender their claims to spiritual absolutism and the exclusive franchise of the purported Vicar of Christ.

The problem is part of a much wider one that Protestants have faced since Vatican Two. It is desirable, even impera-tive, not as a matter of tactics but of Christian conscience and good will, to respond to the new mood and genuine expressions of Christian love. But is it wise to allow Rome such influence in the ecumenical movement that progress is possible only on its terms and subject to its veto? As in the case of the new bodies with Roman participation which replace the British and Scottish Councils of Churches, it may even be necessary to allow the official Roman partici-pants to insist very publicly that the new system depends on member-Churches having the right and even duty to uphold their internal discipline. If Protestants are honest with themselves, they may conclude that the more Rome's discipline on some matters can be subverted the better.

It is not a case of inciting people to rebellion – that wouldn't work anyway – but of welcoming it when it happens and responding to it, just as we should welcome the more positive attitudes to mixed marriages and even inter-communion which are apparently possible within the law of the Roman Church as interpreted by authorities in some other countries, for example France.

That is why, at the grave risk of shocking some of my conservative fellow-Protestants, I cannot condemn those leaders of the Church of Scotland (or even those more obscure ministers) who have joined in a Communion service presided over by a Roman Catholic priest. I deliberately avoid calling it a Roman Catholic Communion service or the Mass. The first of these phrases seems to confer on Church authorities proprietorial rights which belong only to the Head of the Church, from whom they can never be alienated. The second stirs, not least in myself, emotions, convictions, and traditions profoundly related both to the experience of the Reformation and the defence of its insights and inheritance. Besides, if the wrath of one small Presbyterian denomination can fall on an eminent Lord Chancellor and gracious Christian for merely attending a funeral or requiem mass, what indignation awaits an ex-editor from a more free-and-easy Kirk who condones actual participation? That is the extent of my offence, for I have never faced the situation or received an invitation to be more than a spectator at a Roman mass; and until I do I cannot be sure what my response would be. I suspect my conscience would be uneasy whatever I did, and I retain the gut-suspicion not just of the 'blasphemous fables' surrounding the Roman mass — I remind readers that I quote no Presbyterian formula but the Thirty-nine Articles again — but of the very name. For example I found it quite disconcerting when I discovered that Norwegian Lutherans apply it as a matter of course to their Communion services, at which they make visitors most welcome.

But I dwell on the matter, and on events which are probably still uncommon, because they appear to me to go to the heart of the matter of the Protestant future, which involves our attitude to the rest of Christendom — Roman,

Orthodox, heretical sects, and unorthodox African independent Churches. It involves how we ourselves respond to unexpected evidence of the power of God and to inspired independence which has something in common with the elements of rebellion in the Reformation.

Here is how one such case was put to me. Two Protestants are staying in a guest-house in Rome run by Dutch Roman Catholics, probably nuns. They are invited to a Communion service. The president (a priest, of course) invokes the words instituting the Lord's Supper and follows a service scarcely distinguishable from that of the English prayer-book or a Scots Communion order. He recognises the Lord Jesus as the only Head of the Church. He preaches briefly, but with what seems the authentic Word of God. He makes clear that he is no more than a presiding officer and that the celebration commemorates the only and sufficient sacrifice on the Cross. He asks no acceptance of any theory of what happens in the sacrament but invites everyone to celebrate God's grace and take the gifts of bread and wine. 'This is for you.'

Are we to respond by asking him to assure us that he renounces the errors of the Council of Trent? There were many, but at this moment they may not seem the greatest thing in the world. Or by avoiding any decision, like those canny Athenians who told Paul on Mars Hill that they might hear him again? Or by asking him if he has cleared his offer with the proper ecclestiastical authorities? I doubt it.

I do not know what I would now do in such circumstances. I would perhaps be guided by an authority higher than those who draft regulations in any Church. But I am sure that the problem or opportunity or whatever one calls it is going to become more frequent. It is going to provoke argument within the Roman Catholic Church as well as among Protestants. Indeed I have had an eye-witness account of an argument of considerable vigour between the liberal Continental line and the ultra-conservative Scottish Roman Catholic one at a theological consultation with Reformed representatives: not over the theory but over the response to a prospective communicant.

Rome of course makes its rules and gives its provinces and even (in 'emergencies') its priests some discretion. A strange case has been reported in London, for example, of an Anglican clergyman admitted to Communion along with his Roman Catholic wife at his daughter's first Roman Catholic Communion – a situation further complicated by the Anglican claims that she belonged to both Churches and the Roman Catholic one that she couldn't! The Roman rules – for the whole of the Pope's Church – that I have been shown could conceivably be construed to permit this. But the cheerful admission of all the visiting Protestants to Communion at a 'mixed' wedding in Paris – a case told me by a participant – seems to fall outwith the Roman rules. Nor do the rules as I was given them seem at first sight to provide for the inter-communion which I am told by other sources is regarded as legitimate at authorised inter-confessional theological conversations.

I suspect the rules are going to come under more strain and that exceptions, dispensations, even little private rebellions will become more frequent. We shall have to see where the Holy Spirit leads, not just what is said in the small print.

12

DIVERSITY AND ACRIMONY

The weakness and the strength of Protestantism lie close together. Sometimes they are hard to distinguish. Diversity is an asset. It clearly existed in the New Testament Church from very early times. But so (as even a cursory reading of the Book of Acts and Paul's Epistles makes very clear) did harmful divisions and even acrimony.

Any Scots Presbyterian knows the difficulty of deciding just which matters don't enter into 'the substance of the Faith', but the problem is not merely a local one nor an internal difficulty of the Presbyterian parts of Protestantism. For example it is clear that in the next century both the Roman Church and the Orthodox Communion are likely to have more healthy diversity than ever before and a good deal of harmful internal division as well.

We may not think today that the arguments for weekly or twice-yearly Communion enter into the substance of the Faith, or the arguments for commissioning regional officers called bishops or those for and against infant baptism for children of Christian families. At least most of us don't. Some people can still work up considerable passion over such matters. And to some liberal Roman Catholics, who accept the papacy as a symbol of their tradition and sense of a universal, apostolic Church but without any great enthusiasm and with some mental reservations about particular dogmas, it seems surprising and unreasonable that Protestants should still make the rejection of papal claims a matter of Christian principle, very much of 'the substance of the Faith'.

But it is. The papacy is an institution of great historical fascination and complexity, constantly changing and evolving. It has had its triumphs and tragedies, and its grotesque parodies of Christianity. As a notable newspaper used to say of rather different matters, 'All human life is there'. But to the Protestant it must seem a remarkable creation of human ingenuity and no more. A good man may be Pope — and there have been far more good men than evil men on the papal throne — but that goodness confers no special authority, far less infallibility. Christian authority, and the delegated powers of Christ which Churches of all complexions have so often abused, rest elsewhere: in Scripture interpreted in the light of faith, obedience, intelligence, and knowledge; in Christian conscience captive to the Word of God; and in Christian experience guided by the Holy Spirit. Moreover Christian history questions rather than reinforces the claims of the papacy. Rome's later claims were not recognised in the apostolic Church and the kind of authority now claimed for the See of Rome has never been universally recognised in the Church.

Indeed the trend of Roman argument, and of crypto-Roman speculations in other Churches, no longer sets all that much store by imaginative interpretations of the apostolic role of Saint Peter. Instead we are offered a subtler argument after Vatican II about primacy within collegiality, even the pragmatic use of a remarkable existing institution which provides a focus of unity for a large part of Christendom. But that argument fails two tests. The less important, though still formidable, is that a Protestant submission on grounds of expediency would fail in its purpose. It would not give the universal Church a visible unity, for the lesson of Christian history is that God uses and at times even encourages the awkward and the spiritually rebellious. New expressions of Christianity would certainly emerge outwith the structures of 'organic unity', even in the improbable event of Orthodoxy accepting a supremacy that for centuries it has rejected. And any Protestant Church (including the Anglican Communion) which accepted any form of Roman primacy would almost certainly find itself torn apart in the name of unity.

More important still, the Protestant conscience would rebel — just as the Presbyterian conscience almost everywhere rejects the Anglican pattern of episcopacy when offered in the name of unity — against the argument that something should be accepted not because it is right but because it is there.

Yet the survival of different patterns within the universal Church, like the emergence of strains within historic denominations and great differences of approach within the Roman Church, makes it imperative that Christians should seek 'communion in each other's gifts and graces' and speak softly when they differ in love. Unfortunately the history of the Church, from the first century to our own, shows how hard it is to achieve that. There is no clear and well-marked frontier between healthy diversity and harmful divisions, whether in the old arguments between East and West or Protestant and Roman, or in the modern acrimony between liberal and 'fundamentalist'.

These difficulties are especially acute in the arguments

over the role of women in the Church. Today these most obviously divide and embarrass the Anglican Communion and especially the Church of England. It not only finds itself divided but unable to give full recognition to the ministry of women ordained in some other Anglican provinces, including the Church just across the Irish Sea with which it was itself for a time united. At least for the time being it has got into the absurd position of regarding episcopacy as the symbol of the Church's unity yet finding itself unable to welcome a couple of overseas bishops as presiding officers at Communion services. But these divisions extend much more widely. They lie beneath the surface and loom ahead for the future even in the Roman Catholic Church. They will eventually afflict the Orthodox. And they divide Protestantism and not just its Anglican section, not only emphasising some denominational frontiers but widening the gap between ultra-liberal and arch-conservative. They also cause problems for Churches which have gone into the 'liberal' camp but face anything from restlessness to powerful reaction in their conservative sections.

For example the Irish Presbyterians have agreed on guidelines to recognise 'conscientious objection' on the conservative side. Candidates for the ministry will not be rejected because they have theological scruples about women's ordination and ministers may opt out of ordination services for women, though with no power to veto decisions of Church courts. This is a small but fairly important Church which ought to be a bridge between conservatives and moderate liberals. But the bridge may bring troubles from one Church to others.

In the Church of Scotland some conservatives would like the same provision for tender consciences while some liberals would like to close the loopholes which exist in practice where ministers, elders, and their congregations agree not to have women on Kirk Sessions. (The only case so far of a minister apparently forced out of his parish on the issue – not from the ministry – took the form it did because he was at odds with local opinion and not because he dissented from the opinions expressed in Church law.) And in the troubled 'continuing Presbyterianism' of Australia an ultra-conservative reaction threatens to reverse the decisions, made before the division into Uniting Church and continuing Presbyterians, to admit women as ministers and elders.

So much attention has been concentrated on the distress on the Anglo-Catholic wing of the Church of England that other important divisions have been overlooked. In the Church of England the issue is one that also divides the evangelical Protestant wing, just at a moment when it is both necessary and possible for Anglicanism to assert its fundamentally Protestant character. Even more important, the issue is one that divides Protestantism in general, not neatly into liberal and conservative wings but in ways which create confusion and acrimony. Conservatives find themselves forced into strange company if they support or even accept the ordination of women. If they oppose it they may find themselves in practice using harsher words about old friends and allies than about those with whom they disagree on a far wider range of issues.

But it is an important issue, and one with implications that go beyond the immediately obvious matter of whether the sexual equality now accepted in secular society, politics, and employment is to be mirrored in the Church. For the argument about women's place in the Church inevitably becomes one about the Bible's role in the Church and the nature of ministry and ordination. It is also one which brings out a problem which affects both Protestants, who affirm the right of private judgment, and Roman Catholics who belong to a more authoritarian Church in which nevertheless people cannot be stopped thinking for themselves. As we see in the Anglican disputes and the restlessness among conservative Presbyterians, the practical politics of this theological and biblical issue involve the relationship of the individual Christian and his or her community. Should a women who feels a call to the ministry which her Church cannot sustain move to another part of the Church? Some Presbyterian women did so in days when their Churches didn't ordain women but (for example) Congregationalists did. Far more seriously, some Anglican and Roman Catholic women – including one very able theologian in a Scottish university – have moved away from Christianity because it seems so 'patriarchal'. Others have worked to change Church attitudes and systems from within, just as some male conservatives are ready to do in predominantly liberal Churches.

There are therefore three important issues raised directly or indirectly by the 'women's ordination' argument. They are the nature of biblical authority, the biblical basis for ordained ministry, and the relationship of individual conscience and corporate loyalty. Perhaps there is also a fourth: the extent to which Christians may legitimately use experience of God's modern dealings with them to interpret what may seem perplexities in Scripture.

It is not for the amateur theologian to lay down the law on these points. Some of the professionals have caused quite enough trouble. Nor is it for him to usurp the scholar's role and explain the mind of St Paul in the cultural context of his time. But he cannot avoid the implications of the act of faith which enables him to say that the Bible contains the

Word of God, and more than that, contains the Word of God in such a way that it is itself the Word of God. That surely makes it necessary to respond to it in ways which are consistent with its teaching, given the example of Christ (who is the Word made flesh) and the assistance of the Holy Spirit.

Here, therefore, are some suggestions about that response in a matter so important to the Protestant future — important because it divides Protestants and because these divisions have implications for other Christians. In time such considerations will almost certainly come into the thinking of the Roman Catholics and the Orthodox. If the papacy could stumble on so open-minded a tenant as John XXIII in one century who knows what trend a debate might take under some unknown successor-but-three in the next century?

First, those who profess to love God and follow Jesus need to be forbearing with each other. Some of those who are most eager to apply St Paul's rules to modern women in the Church are not at all inclined to be very gentle in setting right those whom they claim to have 'overtaken in a fault'. The most obvious guidance about the right mood is perhaps found in Galatians 6 — it surely does not apply only to the grosser sins — but this is yet another case where the Gamaliel test should properly be applied: if what is being planned and done is of human origin it will collapse. If it is the will of God, however, it cannot be overthrown. But the need for tolerance (within Christian limits) and mutual forbearance extends both ways. It is foolish (for it needlessly emphasises divisions) as well as unchristian to try to provoke test cases or to impose a legalism in those Churches whose majorities have secured legislation making both sexes equally acceptable for ordination, whether as ministers or elders. The force of Church law should surely only be invoked where all attempts at conciliation and pastoral guidance have failed and where local conflict threatens to do worse harm than legal processes. Translated into simple and practical terms for the Church of Scotland and similar Churches (and perhaps as a good guide to future handling of Church of England matters) that may mean: where there is no local conflict do not force the issue and leave well alone, even if a minister and his congregation act as if the law of the Church had never been changed to allow sexual equality.

Secondly, look at all the evidence and guidance of the New Testament and not only the most quotable parts of it. There are conservatives who do in relation to the women's ordination argument exactly what they condemn in liberals: they pick the bits of the Bible that suit them. The New Testament in general, and even the particular phrasing of St Paul in places, suggests that in this as other matters there may have been considerable variety of early Christian practice. St Paul had no doubt good reason for the admonitions he gave particular people, and perhaps he had particular women in mind who were a menace to the Church. Clearly he also had a general principle in the matter, even though he shared in the extraordinarily open and equal approach to women's rights which the early Church displayed, in contrast to its cultural setting. But would he insist on the same general rule today any more than he would suggest that his advice to Philemon about Onesimus should guide us towards legal tolerance of slavery? I suggest the New Testament evidence, taken on its own, leaves the matter at least an open question.

We know, for example, that Phoebe was a deaconess (Romans 16:1–2) at Cenchreae, only a few miles from troublesome Corinth. The Revised English Bible renders her title as a 'minister of the Church' (for a minister is a servant). A couple of verses later Priscilla is recognised by Paul as a 'fellow-worker' and if Junia is a woman (as seems likely) he calls her an apostle. Like Luke in Acts he has no doubt about women's role as 'prophetesses', for Philip the Evangelist had four unmarried daughters in this branch of ministry. Paul lays down rules to the Corinthians for the regulation of women while prophesying which are an explicit acceptance of their right to this role, if called by God. We do need to use only arguments about the social and cultural context of the time to show that the New Testament, while finding divine authority for the role of woman as wife and mother, gives women spiritual equality and a share in leadership. Indeed it gives far more authority for Christian women to claim to be called to a ministry by God than it does for Christian men to claim the special rights and powers subsequently attributed to priests and Popes.

It is clearly arguable, by those who find very direct guidance in the New Testament about the modern structure of a teaching ministry, that there is a problem of conscience over 'teaching elders' (though clearly Christian women teach not only in the home but in Sunday schools and Christian education generally). It may even be possible to stretch Paul's arguments about the relation of husband and wife to raise difficulties about having women as ruling elders. Those who take the ultra-conservative position cannot be coerced in conscience, though they owe it to other Christians to ask themselves how far their views reflect a mere social conservatism. And it may be expedient that for the moment different sections of the Church should have different rules, allowing those with troubled consciences either way to move to a different apartment of the household of faith if they feel any compulsion to do so.

But there are two other factors which I suggest must be taken into account and which for me ensure that women's ordination is not only acceptable but positively desirable. I only ask those those who disagree to ensure that they are taken into account as they surely deserve to be. They have a very direct bearing on the Protestant future, whether in terms of future concord among Protestants of different schools or the influence Protestant Christianity exerts on the secular world and the rest of Christendom.

One is the need to avoid stretching and at times distorting the New Testament evidence to provide a bogus divine authority for purely human patterns of Church organisations. We know how a cheerful pun which Jesus made about Peter's name – still very evident in Latin languages today, though not in English – has been misapplied and knitted into dubious evidence to provide a biblical and historical foundations for the very human power-structures of the papacy. Are we on any more solid rock of history and doctrine when we relate apostles, bishops, ministers, priests, and elders as the Churches have them today to the patterns of the early Church? That those chosen by Jesus had a special standing before God and man is beyond doubt; that there was at least one co-option to fill their ranks, with a further special commission for Paul, is a matter of historical fact. But that the New Testament provides us with a rule-book for the priesthood, ministry, eldership, or prelatical episcopate is open to very reasonable doubt. In any event, women have been part of the true priesthood of the Church since its foundation and women, even in very conservative Churches, have found roles of service and teaching which, though consistent with some New Testament patterns, reflect a very different cultural approach.

Is it an affront to conservative biblical Christianity to suggest that God has laid down flexible guidelines for his Church rather than a rigid pattern? I think not. And as a Protestant I draw a warning from Christian history about all systems which are so rigid and authoritarian that they demand a special caste to operate them and supervise their evolution with carefully defined limits – part of the definition being that the caste privileges be secured!

But Christian history is full of encouragement as well as warnings. The other consideration which I commend as part of a temperate and conciliatory approach to the problems of women's ordination is a response to history, experience, and example, and especially the comparatively recent history of women's ordination. Almost all those opposed to women's ordination – at least in my experience – recognise the commitment, integrity, and often spirituality of women ministers already ordained. It must be very difficult to do that and still believe that these women – together with women elders and Anglican deaconesses who often seem to be doing ministers' work – are not truly responding to a call from God or are all mixed up about it. In the Anglican case deaconesses may have in effect the cure of souls and leadership of parishes. To allow them that, yet seek to deny them the administration of the sacraments, smacks not of conservatism but of a sacramentalism tinged with traces of magic and good deal of superstition.

I don't suggest that those with conscientious scruples, and especially conservative Reformed Churches which are content with their patriarchal rules, should rush to ordain women. But I have enough respect for them to recognise that they will find themselves adding a theological courtesy to their personal one in the dealings that they will increasingly have with women serving in the ministry and eldership of other denominations. I hope such arch-conservatives will not take offence if I suggest that they are being carried by the currents towards dilemmas similar to those that confront the Roman Church in its future dealings with Protestants. Our ecclesiastical bodies are not (say the Romans) parts of the Church in the fullest sense; yet even from the Roman viewpoint they display the signs of the Faith and the marks of the true Church in belief, worship, community, and service. Even a sacramental role is accepted when a Protestant baptism is recognised and some Roman Catholics are (as we have seen) ahead of their Church in their ecumenical approach to the Lord's Supper. In the same way many of those who resist the movement towards the full acceptance of women will find their theories at odds with their experience. Don't these women – few of whom are feminists in any aggressive sense – show the signs of a distinctive kind of Christian commitment, whether to the ministry of Word and sacrament or to sharing the rule of the Church? When they teach from the pulpit do they teach less effectively than in a Bible class?

There are some women, especially extremists among 'feminist theologians', who arouse legitimate fears among conservatives. They are so concerned with sociological theories of male or patriarchal domination that they revolt against the unique and deliberate revelation of God in Christ, who was made man, and reject the metaphor and imagery of divine fatherhood which is itself part of Christ's teaching and God's revelation. This revolt goes inexpressibly far beyond botching up the language of hymns in the name of inclusive language or even slipping in their own intrusive language about the 'motherhood of God'.

140

Those women who combine intellectual integrity with a feminism which rejects or challenges the uniqueness of Christ have to drop the claim in any sense to be Christian. But there are not many of them, and they are not the kind of women who in far, far greater numbers feel called by God to roles which were once the prerogative of men. Let Christian experience, charity, and mutual respect for troubled consciences help to test these calls. I have no doubt that these calls are upheld and that their example will influence not only the ultra-conservative Protestant Churches but the future debate in the Roman Catholic Church and (some day) the adjustment of Orthodox tradition to a changing world.

It is because a temperate, thoughtful, and responsive approach to these difficulties among Protestants can set an example to the rest of Christendom that I have given them a good deal of space. Protestantism has always been a liberating force — whether in its rejection of clerical celibacy, its approach to science, its reconciliation of faith and intellectual freedom, its reconciliation of liberty and order in politics, and its concept of partnership in marriage. Its values survived the French Revolution and should inspire the reaction against the Russian Revolution. It has also its role to play, again reconciling liberty and order, in coping with the sexual revolution which may be more important in the world's history than either of the other two.

That is a personal view which will not carry all readers with it — indeed one of so many personal views that I think it is time to stand aside for a chapter and bring in a few other opinions about the Protestant future.

13

IS PROTESTANTISM OBSOLETE?

I don't think it is so much a Protestant characteristic as a personal one that forces me to see both sides of the question. It is a great weakness, or at least I have found it so not only in politics but in religion. If I were of the Pope's persuasion I would want to know where to apply for a job as devil's advocate.

But the functionaries given that popular title (in, I think, the Roman Congregation of the Causes of Saints) actually hold the title of promoters of the faith. Their critical examination of the alleged virtues and miracles of 'candidates for sainthood' — a procedure at odds with every Protestant instinct — has the merit of good intentions. It is meant to insure against excesses of enthusiasm and naivety. And it brings the comforting thought that in raising awkward questions you may still seek to promote the faith.

In that spirit I posed two questions where I think I wanted reassurance that my own answers were not simply the result of emotion, offering them to a rather haphazardly chosen group of Protestants of different backgrounds and opinions who, for one reason or another, had earned my respect. If the choice was haphazard, the response was even more so. I never heard from some of those from whom I expected strong opinions by return, and one or two of my long shots found a worthwhile target.

The opening question of the devil's advocate is his obvious retort to the title of this book: 'What future?' At the very least it can be questioned whether the Churches of the Reformation tradition have any coherent and distinctive witness to offer, for much of what is said by their governing bodies and their leaders often seems to lack coherence and distinctiveness. For example, Moderators of the Kirk's General Assembly have drifted into the increasingly bad habit of signing statements described as by 'Church leaders'. It is self-evident that if, say, Archbishop Thomas Winning of Glasgow is a co-signatory the statement cannot express any distinctively Protestant view.

The mainstream Protestant Churches, for example in their participation in the World Council of Churches or in national councils of Churches, also often give the impression that anything distinctively Protestant must give way to the needs and styles of the ecumenical movement. For example, the line taken on public issues by the World Alliance of Reformed Churches generally seems no more than an echo of that of its neighbour in the Geneva Ecumenical Centre, the WCC.

But there is a second question which the devil's advocate has a duty to ask. Is the apparently widening gap between liberal and 'fundamentalist' styles of Protestantism now a more significant division than those between historic denominations and confessions?

Does Protestantism have a future, and where does it lie? Is the very word an obsolete concept? These were the questions, with the reasoning behind them, which I put to my panel. The replies were helpful and encouraging, not least because they suggested that a stronger sense of Reformation inheritance and of the Protestant future survives among both liberals and conservatives than is often apparent from their day-to-day comments and controversies.

Take for example the responses of two of those who gave me longer replies than most, but had important things to say from very different viewpoints. John Stott is a commanding figure in the evangelical wing of the Church of England, director of Christian Impact (previously the London Institute for Contemporary Christianity), and now rector emeritus of All Souls, Langham Place. It was he who at the time of controversy about the papal visit planned for Britain in 1982 coined the wonderful phrase, expressing Christian truth and love at the same time, that the Pope should be welcome 'as John Paul, but not as Peter'. Ronald Ferguson, who recently became minister of Britain's most northerly medieval cathedral, St Magnus in Orkney, is better known for his leadership of the Iona Community and his biography of its founder, Lord MacLeod.

John Stott's view is especially important in the light of the Church of England's historical sense of being both a Church of the Reformation and of 'Catholic' tradition:

I have a lot of sympathy with those who urge that we must not refight sixteenth and seventeenth-century battles in the twentieth and twenty-first centuries. For certainly the theological debate has moved on, new issues have arisen, and the old ones need to be reformulated. Nevertheless we cannot put the great Reformation issues on one side by declaring *tout court* that the protagonists misunderstood one another. Some degree of mutual misunderstanding is doubtless present in all controversies. But the issues which were clarified at the

Is Protestantism Obsolete?

Reformation were real and vital issues. They are still burning questions today, particularly because they relate to the crucial areas of authority and salvation.

It is neither compatible with Christian integrity, nor conducive to the Church's health to attempt to sweep such important issues under the carpet by declaring them obsolete. At least those of us who call ourselves 'evangelical', and claim to stand in the Reformation tradition, are determined to maintain *sola Scriptura* in relation to authority, and *sola gratia* in relation to salvation. To be sure, we agree that both reason and tradition are indispensable for the elucidation of Scripture, and that holiness of life is indispensable as evidence of saving faith. Nevertheless we believe that God's redeeming Word and work were finished in Christ, and that any attempt to supplant or even supplement them with human word and works of our own is derogatory to the unique glory and absolute adequacy of the person and work of Jesus Christ.

Thus John Stott. Now Ronald Ferguson:

The notion that anything distinctively Protestant must give way to the needs and styles of the ecumenical movement represents exactly what the ecumenical movement should not be about. 'Protestantism' is not a static concept. Indeed, the Reformers themselves talked about the need for continual reformation — and they would be horrified at the idea of Christians in the late twentieth century repeating exactly what they said. They were far-seeing enough to know that changing circumstances would require changing responses. Protestantism will surely become obsolete or ineffective if it chooses to stay in a seventeenth-century time-warp, or hide in a Victorian pietistic ghetto. It will also become obsolete if it surrenders its distinctive features in favour of some ghastly lowest-common-denominator ecumenical mush.

Two 'Protestant' emphases in particular are essential for the health and vitality of any truly ecumenical movement. The first is the doctrine of salvation through grace by faith. This lies at the heart of evangelical Christian faith, and at the heart of the Reformation itself. It is not only a historical statement – it is the most truly liberating doctrine the world has ever known. The second is the doctrine of the priesthood of all believers – a doctrine which is potentially revolutionary but which is by and large kept under lock and key and only allowed out in the company of a professional trusty.

The radical nature of Protestantism is seen in these two doctrines. Protestantism is at its best when it is radical, free-wheeling, iconoclastic, prophetic, refusing to bend the knee. It is comfortable neither with the political establishment nor with authoritarian prelates. It is democratic in spirit, insisting that the Gospel be expressed in the vernacular, and be accessible to all. When Protestanism degenerates into a prudential buttress for the powers that be, it sells Jesus down the river. If it loses its nerve, and either restricts itself to shouting from the Orange sidelines or singing last century's hymns in a warm glow while the world goes to hell, it will fail the ecumenical movement in its greatest need.

You don't have to agree with all of that – its author would be astonished if I did – to feel its force and relevance, and the way its confronts Protestants and other Christians with their dilemma in face of the powers that be and all human authority, in Church well as State. Powers that are 'ordained of God' — St Paul's phrase — are not to be treated lightly. But there is a role for iconoclasm, and (as the author of Ecclesiastes said long ago) 'a time to break down and a time to build up'. The Scots writer and Kirk elder Angus MacVicar sees this in a rather different way from Ronald Ferguson, though I think part of what he writes may have more direct relevance to the Presbyterian style than to some other forms of Protestantism, which may at times be only too warm and colourful in their style. He says:

> So long as there are free spirits, so long as there are free thinkers who prefer to deal personally with Christ rather than through an agent, so long as spiritual love and not human authority rules the forgiveness of sins, then I believe that Protestantism will endure, though perhaps shedding on the way some of its cold dourness acquired in the wintry days of persecution and allowing more colour and loving warmth to take its place.

I wasn't surprised to get a more conservative view from William Still. To describe him as long-serving minister of Gilcomston South in Aberdeen is correct but quite inadequate. But to seek other descriptions, like leader of the Kirk's conservative evangelicals, can be misleading, for it could imply a formal style and a structure that don't exist. But William Still is both a spokesman and an example for those who believe — in face of attacks on 'fundamentalism' — that a firm stand on fundamentals leads to long and fruitful ministries. They instance 'the departure of great Presbyterian denominations across the Atlantic and in the Antipodes from the historic faith as examples of Churches which might have very little future as advocates of historic Christianity.' The simple statement which William Still offered me on the Protestant future is also a very broad challenge to the Church, and especially perhaps to many of those in various countries and denominations teaching divinity and pastoral theology:

The future of Protestantism, like its past, lies in its faithfulness to the canonical Scriptures, which shall never pass away.

Mr. Still is probably the most influential Scots Presbyterian today who has never been Moderator of the Kirk's General Assembly or wanted to be. I forget how many ex-Moderators I pencilled in for my panel but two of them responded very helpfully. Dr. W.B. Johnston drew my attention to the apparent absence of thinking in print about the future of the Church as seen from a Reformed standpoint, contrasting it with more evident Anglican and Roman Catholic speculation. He also offered me two thoughts from the Anglican Robin Gill's book *Beyond Decline* which ought to influence Protestant thinking about the future. One, from Yves Congar, is about failures which should perplex us. Why have Protestants not convinced others that they 'are the reformed Church'? And why have Anglicans, despite their concern 'to unite Reformed and traditional Catholicism' not made good their claim to be an effective bridge-Church? Bill Johnston also reminded me of the way in which Don Cupitt, whatever else he is, can be stimulating. Is it true that, as Cupitt alleges, Churches are hoarders 'very bad at pruning and discarding obsolete elements' or 'coral reefs which grow by gradual accretion'? There is probably truth in these statements, though not at all where Don Cupitt might think he had found it. The Protestant future involves distinguishing real from imagined obsolesence.

Professor Tom Torrance is, I imagine, even less of an admirer of the Cupitt school of TV Bultmannism — Rudolf Bultmann being a very influential German theologian whose 'demythologising' of the New Testament goes so far as to strain all credulity. It is far easier to believe the original. Professor Torrance's thinking, I believe, will have a significant conservative influence on the future of Protestantism, though he disagrees with many other theological conservatives on the Westminster Confession, maintaining that it puts too little emphasis on the love of Christ. His approach still owes much to his great mentor Karl Barth. However he links one of his great personal enthusiasms and successes — his own work won him the Templeton Prize for Progress in Religion — both with the twentieth-century successes of Protestantism and its future. One of the achievements of the Protestant Churches, he says, has been to take the lead in the reconciliation of science and religion, or as he sometimes puts it, natural science and theological science. For Tom Torrance the Reformed tradition from Calvin to Barth and beyond, influencing the whole Protestant tradition, declares the 'sovereign majesty of the mighty, living, acting, speaking God' in contrast to a more passive patristic and Latin tradition. And 'in Christ the whole electing and covenanting love of God is gathered up to a head and launched into history'.

Tom Torrance often thinks and writes on a plane which it is hard for less gifted souls and amateur theologians to share; but in a lecture at the American Dubuque Theological Seminary in 1988, the text of which he showed to me, he ended on a theme which was a practical as well as a profound guide to the Protestant future. In the development of scientific thinking, he says, Francis Bacon 'took his cue from Calvin' and more than two centuries later the great Scots physicist James Clerk Maxwell successfully brought to his science the 'relational concept of the person' which he found in the Scots Reformed tradition of his Christian faith.

In this century Protestantism may often have seemed unsure of itself, thrown into theological, liturgical, and political confusion, but if the Torrance thesis is accepted it has taken the lead (through scholars of different traditions and denominations, and now in partnerhip with Roman Catholic and Orthodox scientists) in showing that good science and true religion go together.

Finally, to the House of Commons. Alick Buchanan-Smith has a better theological pedigree than most MPs — his grandfather was George Adam Smith, author of the great *Historical Geography of the Holy Land* — but I enlisted him as a voice of intelligent common-sense, a Presbyterian with wide contacts and interests. He calls himself 'a very strong supporter of the ecumenical movement', but one who sees it leading to greater dialogue and co-operation rather than dramatic formal changes. He says:

I do not think that Protestantism in its distinctive form does need to give way to the needs and styles of the ecumenical movement. I think this argument would only be true if there is a genuine merging of the different denominations. However given the very distinctive historical and nationalistic background to the different denominations, I do not see even in the long term a merging of the structures or organisations of the different denominations to any very marked degree.

Is Protestantism Obsolete?

Alick Buchanan-Smith offers a very historical perspective on the point I put to him about the significant gap opening up between liberal and conservative Protestantism.

In a historical sense we have to remember that certainly in the Roman Catholic Church, and now also very apparent in the Anglican Church, there have long been differences of this kind without necessarily threatening the future of those denominations. At times they do indeed cause immense strains and may indeed lead to schism which does occupy the thoughts and activities of the generation in which such differences occur. However the historical viewpoint is very important for institutions which have stood the test of time for many centuries.

He warns that we neglect human nature at our peril and suggests that different beliefs and styles will continue to draw support without the past deep divisions between the Churches.

In this respect Protestantism with its very particular form of government, as well as the emphasis on the role of the laity and the rejection of patronage, will continue for a very long time indeed to come. As a layman I regard that as totally compatible with closer links and co-operation between the different Churches, short of merging.

I add one postscript of my own to these thoughts from various Protestant quarters. The ecumenical movement has allowed itself to be quite disproportionately concerned with the clerical obsession over the 'validity' of orders. I would suggest that for an experimental period all Churches might agree orders that their inter-denominational relations be conducted by committees drawn solely from lay men and women, with ministers, priests, and professional theologians acting only as assessors and advisers. That is not very good Presbyterian theory and it might seem the end of the world in some other denominations. I fly it as a kite in the hope that it may draw attention to the way in which inter-Church conversations are often dominated by matters in which many participants are too involved personally and professionally to achieve much objectivity.

14

LORD OF THE FUTURE

The one title I cannot use for this last round-up of prospects and hopes is 'epilogue'. This has more than a hint of a long sleep about it, and Protestantism needs to come awake. It lives and it will survive, in its ideas, its structures – changed though they may be – and its values. Grace is at the heart of the Christian Faith, and grace is in Christ. He is not a memorable figure in the past of our civilisation but the Lord of the Future. There is abundant evidence in the twentieth century of amazing grace, and of the commanding power of the Jesus Christ of the Gospels. In the theologians' phrase we are justified by faith only. In other words, our good works and good intentions count for nothing but God's grace counts for everything. That discovery is not confined to Protestant Christianity but it is the essence of the Reformed Faith and not merely its inheritance from a distant Reformation. It is a discovery constantly being made as the Word of God speaks to modern humanity. The Church exists to proclaim that reality and gather together those who realise it. There will be a Protestant future while that is preached and shown in the life of the Church as an institution and of its people.

It is no service to God or his people, however, to offer false hopes and suggest brighter prospects, in terms of worldly standing, progress, and influence, than can realistically be anticipated.

But realism is not everything and it is never enough. Who predicted in the Brezhnev era how great a change would come over the Soviet Union? Who in the autumn of 1989 could foresee that by the New Year the hard-line Communist régimes of Czechoslovakia and East Germany would have been swept away? Christians have to reckon with prayers which are answered in unexpected ways and sometimes with unexpected suddenness. We have always to reckon with the unexpected. The Old Testament prophet Habbakuk is not in the top twenty Bible passages today but there is a place for his vision of the appointed time: 'At the destined hour it will come in breathless haste. It will not fail. If it delays, wait for it; for when it comes will be no time to linger.'

But it may be helpful to press some of the ways and calculations of the world into the service of God. If we assess the outlook for Protestantism with our God-given powers of reason and ability to assess evidence, we can draw up a profit and loss account and see strengths and weaknesses more clearly, appreciating the strengths better and facing up to the weaknesses. Then we can view the results in the perspective of our faith. However inadequate and faltering that may be we shall then have a still clearer picture and perhaps a stronger sense of where God may be leading us.

By the standards of this world it is a variable and uncertain outlook, especially in the old heartlands of Protestantism in Northern Europe and North America. Almost all the large Protestant Churches seem likely to decline in statistical terms, whether because of a failure to recruit younger members or because nominal members slide into total apathy. In Scotland, for example, the Kirk would have almost to treble its recruitment of new members to maintain its numbers, such is the demographic pattern.

In the United States the 'white Anglo-Saxon Protestants' – though these WASPS have a strongly Celtic strain – are likely to diminish as a proportion of the population, as are their equivalents in Canada and Australia. In England there are flickering possibilities of statistical revival from a very low point, and more encouraging signs of a much stronger evangelical presence in the Church of England (though Dr. Carey will almost certainly feel pressures at Canterbury to make him adopt a more central position). On the other hand the divisions in the Church of England, especially those over women's ordination, may encourage the drift of higher Anglicans towards Rome or (though less conspicuously and in even smaller numbers) to Orthodoxy.

In Continental Europe Protestant Churches tend to be low in evangelical temperature where they have been traditionally the majority religion. Where they are minorities they feel susceptible (as in other countries) to the Roman Catholic pressures over mixed marriages, even where the hard line has been relaxed. This has been a major factor, for example, in the decline of Protestantism in the Irish Republic. In Britain and Western Europe immigration is also likely to create a more plural society in which the proportion of Protestant Christians may decrease. In France Islam has replaced Protestantism as the second largest religious group.

In Britain there are far more Muslims than Methodists, even though Caribbean immigration has brought new and vigorous strains of Pentecostal Protestantism and British

Asians, like American ones, include evangelical minorities. Moreover Western Europe and North America are likely to encounter new waves of immigration from Central and Eastern Europe, with a relatively small proportion of Protestants among them. These demographic factors also offer opportunities, such as the growth of Protestant Christianity among American Hispanics, the contribution to Church life of Christian Koreans, and even the encouragement of Chinese expatriate congregations which can have an influence on their homeland. But it is realistic to think that this movement of peoples may weaken the social and cultural role of the Christian Churches in the West and affect the mainstream Protestant denominations more than the Roman Catholics. All the Western countries look like becoming both more plural and more secular societies.

But Europe and North America are not the whole world, and the mainstream Protestant Churches are not the whole of non-Roman Christianity. The face of the visible Church is likely to change in several ways as we move to a new century. It will be much less Western, in several senses. For example the Eastern Orthodox Churches may well become more significant if they can respond to the opportunities of what was the Communist world. It will include important elements, even in North America and Europe, of Asian and Caribbean origin. And it will include a greater variety, sometimes a bewildering variety, of Churches in Asia, Africa, and Latin America.

How many Presbyterians, for example, could summarise the range of ethnic and theological shades among the Reformed Churches of Indonesia? How many Christians who have found themselves making political statements about South Africa could describe the beliefs and assess the influence of the various African independent Churches?

'They are heretics and my brothers in Christ.' So a black theological student at Pietermaritzburg once told me. It was a good answer which I am tempted to apply to the College of Cardinals, but only the beginning of wisdom.

Latin America is even more neglected, yet it is probably the greatest growth area of Protestantism today, though the strength of evangelical groups varies enormously from one country to another. Brazil has probably twice as many Protestants as Scotland. 'Born-again Christians' are reported among the quarrelsome politicians and generals of Central America. Sandinista supporters used to tell us that in Nicaragua the Protestants supported the revolution; the other side reported the opposite. Theologians of liberation in the Roman Church in Latin America seem to adopt some very strange interpretations of Scripture, yet they seem to emphasise, even in standing up to the Vatican, a very Protestant right of private judgment and a readiness to encourage the people to search the Bible, even if at times in a questionable frame of mind for Christians.

And what of China where, not all that long ago, Christian visitors found little trace of the visible Church except for a few tolerated congregations of old people and foreigners, and some 'patriotic Catholics', rebels and traditionalists at the same time, who professed to have rejected the Pope but retained Latin? Now we are offered vastly disparate estimates of Christian numbers as well as different opinions about the relation (if any) between an evangelical house church movement and the official Church of the 'Three-Self Movement'. What we do know is that the Church survived and began to revive visibly as soon as persecution was relaxed. We know that Roman Catholicism survives despite the persecution and that it is only for public relations purposes that Protestantism can be presented as a single 'post-denominational' organisation. Yet something new and distinctly Chinese will emerge; and even small minority Churches in the world's most populous country will inevitably have a significant roie in the universal Church.

Trends in the Soviet Union are almost as hard to assess, even though so much information is now available. In a new freedom (or half-freedom) the Soviet Christians themselves are often confused and inevitably divided, not only by denomination but by nationality. The main Russian force in the world Church will be the Orthodox Church, open as never before perhaps to new thinking and outside ideas. But Russian Christianity has a long history of sects and schisms as well as of unquestioning obedience to the powers that be. In the new mood we must be prepared to learn and to help as we can.

What matters is the demonstration that the world's most determined atheist experiment has been a failure – not only as an economic system but as an intellectual and moral one. In the new situation we shall find ourselves working with people, like the Balts, who belong historically to Western culture and with whom we have natural and mutual affinities. We shall also have to work to understand people who have been suppressed under both Tsarism and Communism and who have learned a kind of do-it-yourself evangelical Protestantism. We shall also encounter groups of Christians, like the Russian 'Old Believers', whom we scarcely knew existed.

This assessment is not settling neatly into a profit and loss account, but it should provide some common strands and positive features. First, it shows that the Protestant experience is not something locked up in history, for it is alive in countries and continents on which the Reformation had no direct influence. Secondly, it refutes any suggestion that

Protestantism is necessarily an expression of one economic system or inseparably linked to the liberal democracy of the West, despite the links between them. For it has also taken root in places where it remains to be seen whether Western political attitudes can ever be acclimatised. In Africa for example it is very doubtful whether liberal democracy will take root, though African politicians will speak the language of Western politics and use its slogans, just as they have used Marxist ones. But the Protestant Churches have put down roots in Africa and in the next century ought to find it easier to relate to African traditions and values than Roman Catholicism, unless it jettisons clerical celibacy and follows a Polish Pope fairly quickly with a black one.

In the immediate aftermath of colonialism and in face of the South African dilemma — the attempt by the white minority to create an African nation with European values — it is inevitable that African Christianity should have been associated with ideas of political liberation. In the next century it will face quite different difficulties in face of population pressures, Islam, and probably a revival of traditional African religion.

But despite all the difficulties of transition from mission Churches to indigenous ones, Protestantism is in Africa to stay — and indeed has been naturalised in every continent. That is part of its future. Amid the apparent decline in some places, there will be revivals in the Church moribund, or in parts of it. There will also be new life on what seem the fringes of the institution but are assuredly true parts of the universal or catholic Church.

There are also bound to be developments in other parts of the Church which will probably not be called Protestant but which will express in new ways the discoveries of Grace which we associate with the Reformation and with many evangelical revivals since. Those most obvious to the West will be in the Roman Catholic Church. It cannot read the Bible with impunity. It is seeking ways to express a sense of the shared ministry of all the congregation, which is ultimately the same thing as the priesthood of all believers. Its people will find themselves asking ordained clergymen the question with which, as a good but at times provocative Protestant, I sometimes tease our ministers: 'Are you a priest in a different sense from me?' They will get (as I get) answers which are sometimes plausible, occasionally evasive, but never quite convincing.

There will also probably be changes of Roman practice which narrow the gap in the customs of the different parts of the Church. The most obvious one, which is under way, is the recognition that a sense of full participation in the Lord's Supper cannot be achieved while the vast majority of God's people are denied the cup, with its rich sacramental and memorial symbolism. This change is coming, and while by itself it will not necessarily raise the ecumenically more important matter of inter-communion, it is linked to changes and attitudes which will.

I am sure that Rome is also only at the beginnings of its troubles over sex. The worldly-wise will tell me that it has never been without them, and also that Protestantism (and Orthodoxy in so far as it has married clergy) did not avoid them by making celibacy optional and recognising the chastity of marriage. But these troubles will come with a new intensity and in new forms, for example in two vastly different cultural patterns. In cultures like the modern United States which have a high degree of tolerance of homosexuality it may occur even to some conservative Roman Catholics that the rules – they are not doctrines – which debar from the priesthood men with even moderately strong heterosexual inclinations may have an undesirable effect on the composition of the priesthood. There is already evidence from the Protestant side that some styles of churchmanship attract a proportion of homosexuals well above that in the population generally. The other cultural factor is the difficulty of attracting enough candidates from the priesthood in societies, especially African ones, where men are expected, even more than in the West, to marry. Something of the same problem may explain why after more than four centuries of an intensely Roman Catholic culture Latin America in our century has still been importing priests from Europe and not sending out its own missionaries to modern Spain or France.

Two other apparently unconnected trends may also strengthen the temporarily suppressed urge in the Roman Catholic Church to abandon compulsory celibacy for priests. One is the probability of a trickle of defections from the higher-than-high section of the Anglican Churches as they move steadily towards the ordination of women. The more Rome allows married defectors to remain priests and become special cases, the more absurd it is that some priest and nun should be denied the blessings of Christian marriage to each other because they were born into the Roman Communion. The other trend, which has attracted attention for quite different reasons, is the revival of the Uniates or 'Greek Catholics' of Eastern Europe after their suppression under Communism. They were always there, but they are now more visible, more articulate, more numerous, and more of a factor in Rome's deliberations. They too have married priests, like their Orthodox cousins.

But men have a choice about whether to be celibates. Women have no choice about whether to be women.

Feminist theology, like feminism generally, may run to absurdity and eccentricity but Rome cannot escape its implications or its milder forms. Indeed it seems to have its troubles, in the United States and the Netherlands especially, with forms which run from mild to bitter. In the USA especially it is having to cope with a cultural climate in matters of real or alleged sexism which must seem incomprehensible to most European Roman Catholic prelates.

Rome deserves more sympathy and understanding on this matter than it sometimes gets from liberal Protestants. We must hesitate before alleging that the communion of Teresa of Avila or of the more modern Teresa of Calcutta is hostile to women or does not provide them with opportunities for good works and sometimes great influence. In its recognition of women's talents it is probably closer to Protestantism than either is to Orthodoxy. Even one of the great stumbling-blocks to closer ecumenical co-operation, the place the Roman Church gives to the mother of our Lord in the scheme of salvation, puts Mary, blessed among women, in a position allowed to no man except Jesus himself. We are told she is venerated. We Protestants are expected to stand corrected if we say that she is apparently worshipped, but few of us are convinced by the purported correction. The present Polish Pope has given a new impetus to a veneration which clearly lacks some appeal to modern Roman Catholic intellectuals and liberals. But look at the religion of the people, especially in the popular piety of the Mediterranean countries, where traditional Roman Catholicism remains strong. Mary becomes a necessary mediatrix, a benevolent goddess, the incarnation of mercy and goodness. False doctrine it may be — I believe it is — but it has both a popular and a poetic appeal. The Church which denies women a role in ordained ministry has effectively co-opted one woman as a Fourth Person of the Trinity. The Roman system, far from despising woman-hood, contrives both in theory and in practice to promote popular cults of virginity and maternity at the same time.

But this will not stave off the problem of women in the ministry of all God's people and the priesthood of all believers. The dilemmas which have divided Protestant Churches, separating denominations and (as today with the Anglicans) dividing individual Churches, will appear in the Roman Catholic Church wherever it has to exist in a cultural pattern similar to that of Western Protestantism. This is the world which has learned that women can make formidable Prime Ministers and judges; of equal opportunities and executive aspirations; of Wrens at sea and professors of feminist theology. Of course religion may be excluded from all this as far as the law is concerned. It cannot be excluded from influences and ideas. A few women will drop off the edge of the Church because they cannot thole the idea that God, whom they would call Mother rather than Father, chose to incarnate 'Herself' in a man's body. Far more will conform under various degrees of protest, no more than half convinced by the all-male authority of the Church.

But another few may cause a disproportionate amount of trouble and even ultimately a revolution, for most revo-lutions are caused by determined minorities, not rebellious majorities.

Rome will face the same dilemma as the Church of Scotland in the 1960's and the Church of England today. Once a few women of character and conviction become assured that they have a call to ordained ministry they force the onus of proof – practical, intellectual, and theological – on to those who resist their call. When they are told the

Church knows better than they do they will reply (like Luther) that they cannot back down because their consciences are captive to the Word of God. The very different interpretation they place on that Word from conservative Protestants does not mean that the force of conviction will be less than Luther's; and like Luther and other Protestants they will discover the right, so readily abused and yet in the last resort not to be denied, of private judgment. In very different situations Professor Hans Küng made a similar discovery. So have various apostles of liberation theology and less political souls who simply came to doubt the validity of the semi-divine honours accorded to the papacy. One of the ironies of our time is that the more intelligent and adventurous sections of the Roman Church have been more free-spoken about the aura surrounding the Vatican and its tenants just as the conventional leaders of Protestantism have sworn a vow of silence in the interests of ecumenical diplomacy.

But not all the dilemmas will be on the one side as the Church of the future (meaning the whole body of Christians) seeks to find the will of the Lord of the Future. Even the examples I have suggested of future pressures on and within the Roman Church point to problems for us on the Protestant side.

Our sympathies may be divided and uncertain. The lines of Christian division, not just on minor matters like political theology but on great ones like the nature of the Trinity or the divinity and humanity of Christ, may cut across the denominations instead of running between them. For years I enjoyed the intellectual and theological stimulation of reading the commentaries of the *Monthly Record of the Free Church of Scotland* on the quarrel of the papacy and Professor Küng. The Free Kirk's then editor also wrote a most stimulating book arguing that the Anglicans would probably escape out of the snare of the Roman fowler, but for the wrong reason: they would be determined to ordain women. There are bound to be many more such cross-currents, rather than one strong tide which will carry the Church forward.

There for the moment lies a dilemma for the conservative Protestant, even for conservative Protestants like myself who are ready to welcome women into the ministry and (in Presbyterian Churches) to the eldership. When we look for signs of sunrise over the Vatican we often feel confused. Liberals in the Roman Communion seem to have moved towards our idea of the nature of the Church, if only through their constant assertion of rights of private judgement. But we may find the same people arguing not only for women priests but for homosexual ones, or supporting some singularly nasty Latin American guerrillas, or seeking a synthesis not with Protestantism but with Marxism.

They may even share the approach to Biblical interpretation of such ultra-liberal Protestants as, say, Don Cupitt. But those Roman Catholics whom we find more solid in their views of the Trinity or of society or of sexual morality (give or take a few major disagreements about contraception) tend to have very conservative ideas about those aspects of their Church which we find least acceptable: the authority of the papacy, and not just a primacy; the doctrines of infallibility, Immaculate Conception, and 'Bodily Assumption' which do not belong to the historic and universal catholic faith; the mechanistic view of salvation which has Mary and canonised saints lobbying at the throne of grace; and often a very traditional view of the prerogatives Protestants incline to call priestcraft and of what happens in the Mass (even when said in the vernacular) which opens up a gap between it and any Protestant view of the Lord's Supper.

Nevertheless there are possibilities that in God's Providence and complex purposes both Roman Catholics and Protestants may come to face challenges in areas where Protestants are better equipped to respond. Professor Tom Torrance's thesis about the links between Reformed thinking and the modern reconciliation of science and religion has been mentioned in the previous chapter. Its future importance may extend far beyond Western Christendom as the Russian and other Orthodox Churches emerge from a situation in which atheism had become a kind of State religion. But other areas, involving local church life and pastoral concern, where the Protestant Churches – especially those of the Reformed tradition – should have a head start are Christian marriage and lay leadership in the Church.

There is much common ground among Christians on marriage, and many pastoral difficulties which we have in common. There are also challenges from ultra-liberal elements in the Church or on its fringes which are bound to affect most of our Churches: I was going to say 'all' when I reflected that the Lesbian and 'gay' lobby is not likely to cause much trouble in the Free Kirk.

The time is past when it was possible to contrast the flexibility and hesitancy of the main Protestant denominations on matters of marriage and sex with a constancy, however misplaced and badly defined, on the Roman side. We now face the same pastoral problems, but with the Protestant tradition far better placed to respond pastorally. Rome is handicapped by the gap which has opened up, not just between what the celibate priests say and the people do but between the Vatican line (so powerfully promoted by the present Pope) and the mood and experience of many priests in Western Europe and Latin America. Much Roman Catholic teaching on marriage and family values is admirable – though it goes with such dubious absurdities as annulment procedures which look like divorce – but it is less well placed to help the casualties of a permissive society.

There must also surely be a Protestant future as soon as the whole Church recognises the ministry of all the people of God in its heart and not just with some lip-service. By that I do not suggest that Roman Catholics will turn Protestant in great numbers but that they will turn, consciously or not, to Protestant experience, models, and insights in extending the role of the laity in local leadership, church management, and pastoral assistance. It would be wrong not to recognise the considerable if limited steps that Roman Catholics as well as Anglicans have taken in many places to use their lay Christian talents; and in its new freedom Orthodoxy too is likely to be open to new ideas and opportunities.

Of course Protestants too will find new models. There is likely to be far more debate in the next century than in this one about whether the Church needs an ordained ministry of Word and Sacrament at all. It will be stimulated by the growth of independent evangelical Churches, many of them Pentecostal in style, and by the uncertainty in some of the historic Protestant denominations about the role of the minister. If he (or she) is not going to be a diligent pastoral visitor, and does not preach and teach in a way that conveys authority and carries conviction, sooner or later questions will be asked about whether the role is really necessary. The questions have come later rather than sooner because most historic Protestant Churches, especially the Scots Kirk, retain a remarkable and deeply ingrained respect for the office and dependence, even over-dependence, on its local leadership. Conceivably these attitudes could be eroded under economic and social pressures, though my own opinion is that there will be a revival of the traditional concept of Protestant ministry, with its functions adapted to the place the Church finds in a changed society. I base that belief on the conviction that only men (and women) with a very clear call and strong sense of vocation will choose to be ministers in the next century. However it may be that by then independent Churches with a less clearly defined ministry of Word and Sacrament may account for a rather larger proportion of Protestantism across the world than they do today.

These are the directions in which we seem to be moving and the assets that God appears to have given us. Some of them, like the talents in Jesus' parable, had better not be buried in the ground. For example Churches with a strong tradition of a ruling eldership (such as the Church of Scotland, with its 47,000 men and women ordained to the office) ought to be making more of it. Even there, however, an encouraging feature of the Kirk's life is the serious approach of new elders and the consciousness among elders, old and young, of their inadequacy for the task without guidance.

There are other very obvious weaknesses and failures. In different ways, for example, both Anglican and Presbyterian Churches often seem to have lost confidence in their forms of worship. They complain of 'staleness', yet the attempts at freshness and innovation are at best only partially successful and at worst excrutiating. Anglicanism gave Protestantism a strongly liturgical streak, and anyone familiar with traditional Presbyterian worship will know how often the Book of Common Prayer inspired the language even on our side of the fence. The forms of words which we often find in Anglican services today are a poor channel to communicate the means of grace and the hope of glory. Presbyterianism gave a pre-eminence to the preaching of the Word which depends upon those called to the pulpit – 'twelve feet above contradiction' – having the spiritual depth as well as the intellectual capacity to lead, teach, and inspire the many sorts and conditions of humanity in their congregations. Some of our ministers may not have these qualities, and others lack the confidence to display them.

I am not sure of all the causes, far less the remedies for these conditions. Some of the trouble may lie with the state of the English language, as well as the cultural pluralism which makes it so difficult in musical as well as in verbal communication to find a high enough common factor of participation and response. I am not sure the difficulty is as acute in other Christian cultures. Modern Roman Catholic liturgical English seems to me even more prosaic than what the Anglicans have contrived, but there are parts of the world where the new Roman emphasis on the vernacular must bring some of the freshness that this aspect of the Reformation brought to the worship of the first Protestants. In Spain, for example, one may encounter it not only in sonorous Castilian but in Catalan or Mallorqui. I have also wondered whether the remarkable success of the German Protestant Kirchentag, even if one discounts the evident pleasure of the thousands of young people among the participants in just having a week off school, owes something to a German success of several centuries' standing in integrating music with worship. Perhaps the grass always seems greener on the other side, but modern liturgical German and German church music seem to be under less strain and stress than our equivalents.

Nor can I explain the contrast between the way the German Church draws such numbers of young people into the Kirchentag – a lay movement with a liberal emphasis – and the collapse of so much Protestant youth work in this country, except on the conservative wing of the Church. The main hope for the future leadership of the Church in Britain, national and local, seems to rest quite disproportionately with the disciplines and enthusiasm of the traditions expressed in the Scripture Union and in the Christian Unions in universities and colleges. The collapse, and only very partial rehabilitation, of the Student Christian Movement seems to me to exemplify the way liberal Protestantism has so often slipped into doubt, despair, or diversion into secular causes.

No wise conservative will take any joy in that. Protestantism needs a liberal wing, but (to adapt St Paul's words) it needs to remain part of the one body. That does not mean emphasis on the visible or organic unity of the Church but on the doctrines summarised in the historic creeds and above all on the authority of the Bible. This does not demand any restriction of scholarship or intellectual inquiry, and is consistent with different ways of interpreting Scripture and defining its authority, but it does demand a spirit of reverence and a response to the God who speaks through the Scriptures and whose intervention in human history is recorded there.

I have some sympathy with the very liberal Kirk Moderator with whom I once shared a platform for a broadcast discussion from a Scottish university. It was in the days before the collapse of Marxism and a substantial part of the student audience had come equipped with little red books which they displayed vigorously. The rest of the audience seemed to come mainly from the Christian Union, and waved their pocket Bibles and Testaments in reply. The eminent liberal turned to the university chaplain who was ushering us into this den of rival lions. 'Good grief,' he said, 'have you no ordinary Christians in this university ?'

It may be that the day of 'ordinary Christians' is coming to an end, in the sense that the forms of Christian religion are ceasing to be part of our popular culture and people are no longer necessarily confronted with the claims of God and Christ, whether by preaching, or quiet example, or formal teaching in church and school. I hope not, and I disagree profoundly with those who would retreat from an organised parish ministry and abandon the network of church buildings which in every country of Europe testifies to the Christian roots of our civilisation. There is a role – as there was during the bad times beyond the Iron Curtain – for those who do no more than keep the Church alive while others of stronger will and heart prepare to revive it.

That is a situation in which the different wings of Protestantism need to show more tolerance of each other than they sometimes muster. Evangelicals, including those labelled 'fundamentalist', need to pray for those who seem confused and lukewarm in their faith and yet stay in the Church because they know there is something there that the world cannot provide. In an age when so many social pressures and intellectual fashions encourage the drift away from religious practice those who are strong and certain in their faith should be gentler and more forbearing with those who need help in their half-belief. But the obligation is not only on one side. It is time for liberal professors, bishops, archbishops, and even Moderators of the Kirk's General Assembly to take a vow of restraint, even of silence, when they are tempted to enliven the tedium of their routine duties by criticising 'Fundamentalists'. There are other occasions when Church leaders might be much more positive, for example in encouraging inter-denominational evangelism of the kind associated with Billy Graham, one of the great Christian communicators and publicists of this century. It is a sad fact of Christian life that there is a liberal bigotry as well as the reactionary variety. The Protestant future needs conservatives of liberal outlook and liberals who hold to the fundamentals of the Faith.

But we do not know what God may have in store for us. He is our refuge and our strength, and in Christ, who is one with God, we see God and find God. Many of us also learn after many arrogant failures, stumbles on Hill Difficulty, and excursions into the Slough of Despond, that the question is not whether we in our own time and wisdom will choose God but whether God will choose us.

The Protestant future is what God chooses to make of it, and us. But it is still our duty to try to read the signs of the times. We shall not all see the same signs or read them in the same way, and the Protestant future will be shaped – as some of the thoughts in the previous chapter so clearly indicated – by people with very different interests and opinions. Areas which this book has hardly touched on, such as the intensity of Christian social concern and the quality of Christian social work for handicapped children or the elderly in senile decay, will help the Protestant future as William Wilberforce or the Earl of Shaftesbury helped shape the Protestant past. The concern for the world's social improvement, expressed by Tear Fund and Christian Aid and their equivalents in other advanced countries, also links the missionary tradition to the new relationships of the post-colonial era, though we should not forget that in many parts of the world missions of a more traditional type can still find a role.

But the heart of the Christian experience is not these good works, testimony to faith though they are, but God's call to humanity everywhere to repent, incarnated in the life, teaching, and risen presence of Jesus, Son of God and the Lord of the Future. We are saved by grace through faith. We are also bidden to shine with a pure, clear light.

We shall do so more confidently and coherently if we recover our sense of a common Protestant inheritance and experience. We waste too much time worrying about an organic ecumenical unity which is at present unattainable and fail to explore and enrich the common factors in our Protestant experience as the reformed parts of the universal Church. That is wholly consistent with welcoming the great and beneficial changes that may happen elsewhere — whether in the Roman Church's use of the vernacular, its new enthusiasm for Bible-reading and study, and the genuine open-ness and Christian friendship which many of its people show towards us and which we cannot fail to reciprocate. We have to wait and see where these moods may lead two or three Popes from now, as far as official attitudes are concerned. Meanwhile we can rejoice in signs of grace, as we surely do when the Orthodox liturgy is heard again in the Kremlin. Offer every Russian a Bible and there will be many more reforms to come there, in Church as well as State.

The irony of our times is that the mood and the leader-ship of some of the larger historic Protestant Churches is most confused and even debilitated just as all that Protestantism stands for, and much that it has contributed to the secular world, is being vindicated. The faith has survived and revived even where Church authorities were timid and conformist. Communism is getting a Christian burial. National religious traditions are reasserting themselves. But it is clear that aspirations for personal freedom can only be met in a society that also respects a rule of law. In economics the emphasis has dramatically switched from imposition of Socialism to the moral framework, of personal and corporate responsibility, that is needed in a market economy. Protestantism no longer needs to be ashamed of the historic connection which links it, at least in its West European and North American heartland, to the rise of capitalism. No more need it be ashamed of the strand in Protestant thinking – involving for example Barth, and Niebuhr in his early phase, as well as Keir Hardie or William Temple – which sought a social democracy with a Christian face. In their economics these attitudes are hopelessly dated, but not in their social concern. The failure of Socialism in Eastern Europe and vindication of capitalism in the West makes it all the more important to recover and sustain personal moral values and a Christian-inspired sense of community.

But ultimately Protestantism is not about human values, liberal opinions, or the economics of a free market. It is not about the interplay of human opinions but about the intervention of God in human history and individual lives. It is the ultimate and only true theology of liberation: liberation from superstitious fears, from the emptiness and despair of alienation from God, and from the notion of a caste or hierarchy that regulates salvation and administers a Purgatory; but above all liberation from the sin that is within ourselves and part of our condition. For as St Paul declares with such power in Romans 8, all things will work together for good to those who love God, and nothing will separate us from the love of God which is in Jesus.

The Protestant future is to reflect the Light of the World.

BIBLIOGRAPHY

In a book of this kind a bibliography could be exasperatingly long or short. The only middle way is to make it a very personal as well as a selective one, in the hope that what interested and helped the writer may do as much for the reader. The result is to offer a bibliographical essay rather than a mere list of books. The arrangement does not follow the chapters of this book but where a work is especially relevant to a particular theme this is mentioned. I thought that footnotes would be even more trouble to the reader than to the writer and have omitted them.

For any Protestant bibliography there is only one place from which to start. It has to be with what Protestant Churches regard as the supreme standard: the Bible. For English-speaking readers (or at least Protestant ones) this used to mean the 'Authorised Version' or King James Bible. In a sense it still does, as even when we use some other translation we are likely to compare it with the A.V. We are also almost bound to use the A.V. when we want to quote a biblical phrase that has entered into our culture, religious or literary. The principal alternatives are probably the New International Version, which reflects some evangelical preferences and the most recent significant version, the Revised English Bible (Oxford and Cambridge 1989), itself a revision of the New English Bible of 1961–70. The Good News Bible (British usage edition, Bible Societies and Collins 1976) is the main popular version, in the sense of being the most simplified in language.

There are various New Testament translations which show how, nearly 2000 years after these books were written, and four centuries after the great definitive translations inspired by the Reformation, they can still give literary as well as spiritual inspiration. Among them are J.B. Phillips' *Letters to Young Churches* (Geoffrey Bles 1947) and his version of the Gospels, William Barclay's translation of the New Testament (Collins 1968, reissued Arthur James 1988), and W.L. Lorimer's *The New Testament in Scots* (Southside 1983, Penguin 1985), the last reflecting something of the literary impact that pioneer biblical translation of quality can have in any language.

Readers reasonably fluent in other languages will soon became aware of the cultural impact of biblical translations there too — for example in looking at the German translations based on Luther's work. The equivalents of the Good News Bible will introduce the reader to the continuing vigour of the New Testament in a wide range of languages. The Spanish *Dios Habla al Hombre* (Bible Society, Madrid 1982) is a good example.

SUBORDINATE STANDARDS
Most Protestant Churches have documents with legal or doctrinal authority or of great historic significance. They do not vary as much as might have been expected in view of the quarrels in which they have sometimes been invoked. One thing which they have in common in the twentieth century is that they have not proved easy to revise or replace satisfactorily.

The two most important for the English-speaking world are the Book of Common Prayer of the Church of England (1662) with modern amendments and many derivatives and variations, and the Westminster Confession of Faith. The

Prayer Book (there are modern editions of the traditional book) is the easiest place in which to find the Thirty-Nine Articles of Religion (1571), the basis of the Elizabethan settlement of the Church of England. It is also the basis of Wesleyan Methodist traditions.

The Westminster Confession of Faith (traditionally published with the Larger and Shorter Catechisms) is the principal subordinate standard of the Church of Scotland and many other Presbyterian Churches, though there has been a tendency (most notably in the USA) to relegate it to a historic status along with other great Reformed documents such as the Helvetic and Heidelberg Confessions. Its role in the Church of Scotland is a matter of some ambiguity and dispute. As its title suggests it is not a Scottish document but an English one in which Scots were involved. More detailed study of the Scots Presbyterian tradition involves study of the *Scots Confession of 1560* and the *First and Second Books of Discipline.* There are modern editions. There is a detailed but sometimes critical American commentary on the Confession in *The Westminster Confession for Today* by George S. Hendry (John Knox Press 1960).

REFERENCE BOOKS

Apart from standard encyclopaedias, the reference book which is most helpful in assessing Protestant Christianity is the *New International Dictionary of the Christian Church* (Zondervan 1974 with Paternoster British edition). The *Oxford Dictionary of the Christian Church* (second edition 1974, with concise version only a quarter of the length 1977) is valuable but shows signs of much 'higher' or 'Catholic' views of the Church.

There is much useful material about the contemporary structure and condition of the Protestant Churches in the

Handbook of Member-Churches published by the World Council of Churches (Geneva 1982, later revised) and in the United Bible Societies Bulletin annual reports.

Those who want simple guides to Scripture, especially as it relates to the structures of the Church that have evolved since New Testament times, can find a wealth of biblical dictionaries, some of them with more lexicographer's comment than even Dr. Johnson would have intruded.

Popular high-quality New Testament commentaries include the multi-volume *Daily Study Bible* by William Barclay (Saint Andrew Press, various dates) and the one-volume *New English Bible Companion to the New Testament* by A.E. Harvey (Oxford and Cambridge 1970). Helpful 'heavies' include the *Eerdmans Bible Dictionary* (1987) and the *IVP New Dictionary of Theology* (1988).

HISTORY

There are no neat dividing lines to separate history from theology and biography where the Church is concerned. 'Short histories' of this and that can be quite long and remain superficial. The serious but non-academic reader may be better off using a mixture of good reference books and more specialist books about people or themes of interest. In the case of the great Reformers it is also desirable to get at least the flavour of what, say, Luther, Calvin (in *The Institutes of the Christian Religion*), Knox (in his *History of the Reformation in Scotland*), and Wesley in his diaries wrote, taught,and perhaps incidentally revealed about themselves. There are readily accessible good modern biographies of Luther (by Roland Bainton) and Calvin (by T.H.L. Parker) with Lion editions of both (1987). These indicate the scale of the industries devoted to processing the lives and works of the two greatest Reformers.

Bibliography

There are useful short guides to more recent Protestant theological trends, notably *A Century of Protestant Theology* by Alasdair Heron (Lutterworth 1980) for the age when science made its great impact. *A Handbook of Christian Theologians* (editors D.G. Peerman and M.E. Marty 1965, revised Lutterworth edition 1990) is not confined to Protestants. Those who want straightforward history could try the Lion handbook *The History of Christianity* (revised 1990) and Paul Johnson's Penguin history of Christianity, written from a 'progressive' but not left-wing Roman Catholic standpoint.

Valuable books on the British Churches include two three-volume works – David L. Edwards' *Christian England* (Collins 1984) and the studies of the Scots Kirk between 1688 and 1900 (Saint Andrew Press 1973–78) by A.L.Drummond and James Bulloch. A.C. Cheyne's *The Transforming of the Kirk* (Saint Andrew Press 1983) is of much more than Scottish interest, for it deals with Victorian themes which reshaped all Reformed Christianity. There is scholarship and insight in Gordon Donaldson's classic study of Scotland: *Church and Nation through Sixteen Centuries* (SCM 1960, Scottish Academic Press 1972) and his *The Faith of the Scots* (Batsford 1990). The viewpoint is a rather individualist Protestant conservative Episcopal one. *Scotland: Kirk and People* by Ian Henderson (Lutterworth 1969) is outstanding but inevitably dated on some matters.

ECUMENISM
There is a vast library on the ecumenical movement. The standard *History of the Ecumenical Movement* comes in two very solid volumes (reprinted WCC Geneva 1986) covering 1517–1948 (edited Rouse and Neill) and

1948–68 (edited Fey). There is also a vast library of 'church unity' reports, many of them abortive. A significant recent one is the WCC *Baptism, Eucharist, and Ministry* supplemented by volumes of responses from member-Churches, some of them showing a strong Reformed reaction to the failure to take the eldership and its equivalents seriously. The ARCIC (Anglican-Roman Catholic conversations) reports are important, as is the sour Vatican reaction from the Sacred Congregation for the Doctrine of the Faith (CTS translation 1982). Two sharp but well documented Reformed reactions, with hostile critiques of ecumenism, are Sir Alec Johnston's *Presbyterians Awake* (Saint Andrew Press 1988) and Donald Macleod's *Rome and Canterbury: a View from Geneva* (Christian Focus 1989). Professor Macleod's Geneva is Calvin's parish, not the WCC beat.

ROMAN CATHOLICISM
Literature about the Roman Catholic Church is now as diverse as that on Protestantism. *The Pope's Divisions* by Peter Nicholls is a high-class journalistic introduction (Penguin 1981). A 'progressive' view of the papacy is found in *The Bishop of Rome by* J.M.R. Tillard (translation, SPCK 1983). A refreshing historical book of great relevance is *How the Pope Became Infallible* by A.B. Hasler (translation, Doubleday 1981). Any Protestant who thinks that the Roman Church does not harbour some very free scholarship should read this account of the First Vatican Council, with sympathetic introduction by Hans Küng. There is a useful *Short History of the Catholic Church* by J.D. Holmes and B.W. Bickers (Burns and Oates 1983).

For a taste of the hard line from the present Pope try the encyclical *Redempotoris Mater* (CTS translation 1987). The works of Hans Küng display the other faces of Catholicism, one almost Protestant where the papacy is concerned but another ultra-liberal. The key book on the liberation theology in the Roman Church, which also affects a sector of Latin American Protestantism, is *A Theology of Liberation* by Gustavo Gutierrez (translation, SCM Press 1974). For wider views of Latin America and the history of Protestantism there consult the bibliography of the relevant section in the *New International Dictionary of the Christian Church.*

EASTERN EUROPE AND CHINA
Bibliographies on Eastern Europe are going instantly out of date. Such a valuable book as Trevor Beeson's *Discretion and Valour* is now hopelessly dated. Keston College's journal *Religion in Communist Lands* has a partially obsolete title but a mass of valuable material, for example recording the protests of Laszlo Tökes when still confined to local Church bodies in Romania.

Relatively up to date is the volume on Eastern Europe in the MARC World Christianity series (Eastbourne 1988). Solzhenitsyn's *Gulag Archipelago* and other works contain much of religious importance. At the time of writing the most significant addition to the Keston tradition is Michael Bourdeaux's *Gorbachev, Glasnost, and the Gospel* (Hodder and Stoughton 1990). The same problem of obsolescence applies to China. The *New International Dictionary* bibliography is a good guide to basic historical material. Readers of modern paperback and periodical material will quickly encounter the feud between the supporters of the Three-Self Movement and the more evangelical enthusiasts for the house church movement.

THEOLOGY

The very word 'theology' puts many readers off, but even some book which may seem theology for theologians can be helpful. See for example in T.F. Torrance's *Theology in Reconciliation* (Geoffrey Chapman 1975) some insights into Protestant and Catholic theology and an incisive critique of where the ecumenical movement and especially the WCC falls into secular traps. The same author's *Mediation of Christ* (Paternoster 1983) is, as the title implies, about the centralities of the Faith. Some especially relevant comments on the Protestant future will be found in his 1988 Donnell Lecture at Dubuque, printed in *Incarnational Ministry* (edited Kettler and Speidel, Helmers and Howard of Colorado Springs).

The views which John Stott summarises in chapter 13 of this book have been developed in his extensive writings. He especially mentions his 'dialogues' with David Edwards, *Essentials* (Hodder and Stoughton 1988).

A very different tradition is lucidly developed in *The Gospel and the Catholic Church* by Michael Ramsey, sometime Archbishop of Canterbury (1936, reissued SPCK 1990).

For the rest, the reader can pick and choose, with a special recommendation to skip most of the modern lamentations of 'political theology'. Karl Barth has a permanent importance and the easiest way to start is to read his essay on Mozart (translation, Eerdmans 1986 with introduction by John Updike). Reinhold Niebuhr's most compelling book is still *Moral Man and Immoral Society* (Scribners 1932, subsequent editions) but his opinions moved on. His selected writings in Reinhold Niebuhr: *Theologian of Public Life* (edited Rasmussen, Collins 1989) offer a more comprehensive introduction.

Bibliography

There is an introduction to Orthodoxy for Westerners in the works of Anthony Bloom (Metropolitan Anthony). Edward Schillebeeckx displays some of the changes that have come over Roman Catholic theological thinking in Western Europe.

BIOGRAPHY
Of the making of Christian biographies there is no end. Those shedding light on the future of Protestantism and perhaps raising problems about it include Eberhard Bethge's various books about Dietrich Bonhoeffer, the wartime German martyr, and Ronald Ferguson's *George MacLeod: Founder of the Iona Community* (Collins 1990).

SCIENCE
There are many good modern books about Christianity and science. One which brings out the beneficial influence of Protestantism and especially Calvinist Puritanism is *Religion and the Rise of Modern Science* by R. Hooykaas (Scottish Academic Press 1973).

INDEX

The names of authors mentioned or quoted are listed where they are referred to in the main part of the book and not solely in the bibliography.

Index

Index